For Penny and Mary Ellen

D0170978

Sweet smiling village, loveliest of the lawn,
Thy sports are fled, and all thy charms withdrawn;
Amidst thy bowers the tyrant's hand is seen,
And desolation saddens all thy green;
One only master grasps the whole domain,
And half a tillage stints thy smiling plain.
No more thy glassy brook reflects the day,
But, choked with sedges, works its weedy way;
Along thy glades, a solitary guest,
The hollow-sounding bittern guards its nest;
Amidst thy desert walks the lapwing flies,
And tires their echoes with unvaried cries;
Sunk are thy bowers in shapeless ruin all,
And the long grass o'ertops the moldering wall;
And, trembling, shrinking from the spoiler's hand,
Far, far away thy children leave the land.

Ill fares the land, to hastening ills a prey,
Where wealth accumulates, and men decay.
Princes and lords may flourish, or may fade;
A breath can make them, as a breath has made;
But a bold peasantry, their country's pride,
When once destroyed, can never be supplied.

—Oliver Goldsmith
from The Deserted Village

Contents

Preface   xi

Paradigms of Economic Development and Beyond
     Charles K. Wilber and Kenneth P. Jameson   1

Perspectives on Capital and Technology in
Less-Developed Countries
     Arnold C. Harberger   42

A Basic-Needs Approach to Economic Development
     Paul Streeten   73

An Age of Global Reconstruction
     Celso Furtado   130

Economic Development: A Marxist View
     John G. Gurley   183

Contributors   253

Preface

IT IS WITH PRIDE that we at the University of Notre Dame publish this collection of articles by four of the foremost thinkers in the field of development. The early versions of the papers were presented as part of the New Directions in Economic Development lecture series during the 1977–78 academic year. This is the second such volume. The first published the papers from the New Directions in Public Policy series of the 1976–77 academic year.[1]

The four essays all break new ground or synthesize new departures in development economics. For this reason, we decided to prepare an introductory essay that would place the four works in the context of general development theory. However, as we were writing, it became apparent that a new theme—that of "convoluted history"—was implicit in the essays, and that they definitely push beyond the usual bounds of development thinking. Thus our own essay was forced to look beyond those confines as well. We hope that it provides a useful context for reading the main essays.

We are grateful for the enthusiastic participation and willing cooperation of our lecturer/authors: Arnold C.

---

[1] Frank J. Bonello and Thomas R. Swartz, eds., *Alternative Directions in Economic Policy* (Notre Dame: University of Notre Dame Press, 1978).

Harberger, Paul P. Streeten, Celso Furtado, and John G. Gurley. In addition to their formal papers, they spent many, many hours with our students and our colleagues and, in the process, provided fresh insights into the numerous problems confronting those engaged in the task of development.

Special thanks go to James H. Weaver, the American University, whose ideas have become so entangled with ours that it is no longer possible to sort out ownership. Without the cooperation of the University of Notre Dame Press and particularly of its director, James Langford, this volume would not have been possible.

KENNETH P. JAMESON
CHARLES K. WILBER

Paradigms of Economic Development and Beyond

Charles K. Wilber and Kenneth P. Jameson

I. Introduction

DURING THE MORE than thirty years since the end of World
War II and the founding of the United Nations, "development" has captured the attention of economists and states-
men alike. Of course international inequalities are not new,
but three factors account for this recent emphasis: (1) the
realization that the worldwide spread of markets has not
automatically brought the benefits promised by nineteenth-
century economic theory; (2) the emergence of socialism as
a viable development alternative; and (3) the pressure for
economic development exerted by the newly independent
countries of Latin America, Asia, and Africa with the resulting challenge to existing economic relations. In all of
these cases, the meaning of "development" is a crucial
element.

Theorists and practitioners of development have written
and labored in universities, government agencies, and international institutions. International conferences have been
held, billions have been spent on foreign aid, and thousands
of experts now earn their living from development. However, this prolonged preoccupation has not resulted in a

1

generally accepted explanation of the process of development. Indeed, an initial survey of the field would seem to suggest an analogy with the Tower of Babel. Closer examination, however, shows that there are two main categories of treatments of development, one we will term "orthodox" and the other "political economy."

One of the purposes of this chapter is to suggest how the diverse writings on development can be understood as belonging to these two competing categories. But a second goal is to show that the intellectual strictures which accompany work within either of these two traditions may actually hamper our understanding of development; we must move beyond them to an approach based on what we term "convoluted history." The final section serves as an introduction to the later chapters and shows how they do indeed move beyond the confines of these two main approaches, thereby aiding our understanding of the development process.

The initial problem is to establish the context in which the interplay of the two main approaches is played out. Thus the question of intellectual competition in economics must be considered.

II. Intellectual Competition in Economics

The status of economics as a science has provoked active debate in recent years. Some claim that economics has indeed gained the coherence and explanatory power to qualify as a science, while others claim that it is presently in a prescientific state and is likely to remain there forever. Of course the entire debate traces back to the work of Thomas Kuhn,[1] who in his history of science used the construct of the "paradigm" to show that science and its development are much more complex than the simple march of value-free knowledge which progresses by its own persuasiveness.

There is no need to enter into the debate on the nature of economics nor into the hot philosophical debate sparked by Kuhn. As a device for ordering thinking about economic development, the concept of a pardigm will be useful.

For our purposes a paradigm is a world view shared by a group working on or thinking about a particular topic, e.g., economic development. Such a world view affects their activity across the board: the questions which are asked, the information which is collected, the method of interpretation of that information, and even the group with which there will be communication about the questions. Because of the functioning of this world view and this scientific community, advances in knowledge about the particular concerns of this community are facilitated; but it is very difficult to move from one world view or one community to another. As long as the paradigm relates successfully to the questions addressed, there is substantial "progress" in understanding and knowledge. On the other hand, even when the questions are not addressed with a high degree of success, i.e., when there is a crisis in the community, members of the community continue to follow the paradigm's guidelines rather than breaking with that world view and adopting another.

This paradigm or general theory—whether it be neoclassical economics, Marxism, or some other—is usually so much a part of the very thought process that empirical disconfirmation of some particular hypothesis is almost automatically rejected. There are a variety of specific problems that make it easy in economics to reject a disconfirmation as invalid and thus to protect the scientist's theory or paradigm.

First is the *ceteris paribus* problem. Hypotheses in economics must always be stated in the form of "if . . . then" propositions. Since the "ifs" do change, an econometric test that disconfirms the theory can always be rejected as "misspecified." In addition, since hypotheses are stated in probabilistic terms, a nonoccurrence of the predicted event cannot be used as a refutation of the general law from which the particular hypothesis was deduced.

Second is the difficulty of constructing a clear-cut test of a hypothesis in economics. Most of the traditional statistical tests (for example, null hypotheses) are very weak and a large number of different theories are capable of passing them. The choice among alternative theories, therefore, cannot be settled on empirical grounds. Instead, the desirable qualities of a logical model—simplicity, generality, specificity, and aesthetic quality—are used, and the relative evaluation of these qualities is probably determined by one's own paradigm.

In the area of development—which is multidisciplinary by nature—these problems of verification are multiplied many times over. When a general theory or paradigm has achieved a high level of insulation from falsification it might best be termed an ideology or, less pejoratively, a parable. As parables, both the orthodox and political-economy paradigms of economic development serve two essential and related functions. Each acts to restrict the scope of what is considered "scientific" inquiry and each serves as a policy stance for molding society in its image.

Before turning to specific consideration of the two paradigms, let us indicate in a general manner what the main components of paradigms or parables of development are. It will be seen that a major consideration is the view of history implicit in the paradigm, a theme to which we will return in later sections.

An Outline of Development Paradigms

Both the orthodox and the political-economy paradigms grow out of Western modes of thought, and thus they have similarities in their patterns of analysis and thinking. This fundamental similarity can be seen by going back to the definition of development given in *Webster's Third New*

International Dictionary. Development is defined as "the act, process, or result of developing: the state of being developed: a gradual unfolding by which something . . . is developed: gradual advance or growth through progressive changes." This obviously requires examination of the word "develop," which is defined as "to cause to unfold gradually: conduct through a succession of states or changes each of which is preparatory for the next."

From this we see that development has the implication of a gradual unfolding or of a passing through stages, each of which prepares for the next. When applied to the context of countries existing in time, it shows that development must be dealt with in a historical context. The historical experience will condition the stage in which a country finds itself and the degree to which its development has unfolded.

From the definition, there is another sense in which history is important. To talk of an "unfolding" implies the stripping off of overlays which are hiding the true nature of the subject; it suggests the gradual emergence of the nature of the entity which for some reason has been hidden but which reveals itself with the passage of time. There is in this view a type of teleology, an end to which history is tending or should tend. So development is more than simply change or the passage of time; it is change in some particular direction. Such a stance fits quite nicely with the other definition of development, the passage from stage to stage. As long as each succeeding stage is a "higher" stage, then the process of history and development is again teleological. This can be seen most clearly in the writings of W. W. Rostow on the stages of economic growth,[2] but it also appears in a close reading of virtually any text on development. Thus, Bauer and Yamey talk of "the widening of the range of alternatives open to people as consumers and producers";[3] Higgins sees development as "a discernible rise in total and in per capita income, widely diffused throughout occupational and income groups, continuing for at least two generations and becoming cumulative":[4] Seers says that it must be treated in relation to a "universally acceptable aim—the realization of the potential of human personality";[5] while, finally, Denis Goulet in talking of the French school describes their view as "development itself is simply a means to the human ascent."[6]

Joining together the historical element of development with the teleological, it is rather easy to arrive at a view of history as a parable of "progress" toward that final goal. It is this aspect of development thinking whose philosophical roots are examined by Celso Furtado in the first portion of his essay in this book.[7] In his *Economic Development*, Culbertson[8] points out that "belief in progress" characterized the classical writers and Marx as well as the neoclassical school of development thinking, i.e., that progress is a component of both of the competing paradigms of development. The fundamental role of "history = progress" will be emphasized in the final section of this chapter.

Two other components complete the skeleton of the analytical framework of the two paradigms. The first is their attempt to deal with the continued existence of "underdevelopment." Obviously few if any countries have developed fully, and an explanation for this must be a part of the paradigm. More particularly, why is it that the range of performance is so vast, from that of the United States or Sweden on one end, to a Chad or Guinea-Bissau on the other? Thus, a complete view of development must contain a "theory of underdevelopment" which can provide a plausible explanation for the existing state of events. The second component, naturally, is a "theory of development." In other words, there must be offered some explanation of the mechanism or motive force which moves countries through history in their process of development. It is in the theories of development and underdevelopment that the two paradigms differ most radically.

With this as background, we are now ready for a rapid tour through the two main paradigms of development before turning to an alternative view of history and to the essays in this volume and their contribution to an understanding of the process of development.

III. The Orthodox Paradigm

Development thinking in the United States has long been dominated by what we term the "orthodox" paradigm. Although it has certainly undergone an evolution and has several variants, its basic outlines adequately encompass a majority of the writers on economic development in this country. Following the schema outlined above in terms of its major components, we can sketch out the general outlines of this paradigm.

The basic goal of development has been seen traditionally as the attainment of a "high mass consumption" society, to use Rostow's term. It is understandable, therefore, that orthodox development economists have usually measured the level of economic development by the level of per capita income or product. The implicit goal of development appears to be the creation of societies that replicate the political-economic system of the United States: a private enterprise economy combined with a representative, democratic political structure.

The view of the historical process contained in the orthodox paradigm is clear from this characterization: it is one in which developing societies move toward ever greater availability of goods and services for their citizens. This is the nature of progress, and, as a result, growth in the per capita output of goods and services is often used synonomously with development. Since the general unit of analysis is the nation-state, it is the average per capita income of the whole population of the nation-state that moves to higher and higher levels as the historical process of development continues.

As might be expected, the treatment of this historical process is closely intertwined with the theory of development incorporated in the paradigm. It is often held that development and progress are almost natural and lawlike and that history is simply a continuum from the poorest to the richest countries. The main difference between them, aside from natural resource base, is the time which separates them from underdevelopment.

Rostow's stages-of-growth model is the best known and most explicit presentation of this view of historical development. The use of this model as a framework for analysis of the process of development assumes that present-day countries correspond to the "traditional society" stage or, at best, the "preconditions" stage in the Western developed countries. That is, the present-day developed countries were once underdeveloped and all countries move through all these stages.

How can this development best be brought about, that is, what mechanisms will most surely lead to growth and development? Of course there are a variety of approaches to this problem, but the one which has greatest claim to the orthodox position is the view that development will be facilitated by doing nothing, by letting things alone: "laissez faire."

This view grows out of the model of competitive market capitalism. Since an uncoerced person can be depended upon to act rationally to maximize his/her individual self-interest, it is thought that an automatic, self-regulated mechanism to manage economic affairs naturally emerges in the course of history. These free choices are expected to overcome scarcity and to result in progress through the automatic adjustments of free exchange in markets. The forces of competition ensure that the economy produces those goods which people desire and that maximum output is produced in the most efficient manner.

Since the process is virtually automatic and technically determined, this suggests the theory of underdevelopment. If development has not occurred, then the reason must be that something interferes with this automatic process. The analysis of obstacles to development is, in effect, the theory of underdevelopment contained in the orthodox paradigm. Two examples can illustrate the concept of obstacles. One obstacle to growth may be nonrational behavior, that is, nonmaximizing behavior. Because of cultural dualism,[9] lack of n-achievement,[10] or other social/cultural/psycho logical constraints, people tend to behave in ways that perpetuate traditional forms of economy, and thus retard development. Another is the obstacle to the free working of markets created by government regulation and participation in the economy[11] and by the imperfections of markets caused by the low level of development.[12] These two categories of obstacles hamper the automatic progress of development which otherwise would take place.

The possible existence of such obstacles represents a challenge to policymaking, and two main responses to this challenge have developed since World War II. In addition a third response, growth with equity, has developed in recent years as a reaction to what is perceived as the failure of development programs.

Laissez Faire and Planning Responses

Suggested policies to overcome these obstacles to the automatic process of development have been quite varied. However, they fall into two major groupings: a continued defense of the laissez faire strategy[13] or a belief that substantial government planning will be required to overcome these obstacles.[14]

The laissez faire response is twofold. On the one hand, it questions the observations of nonrational behavior. There is a large literature in the economic anthropology area which finds rational maximizing behavior in widely varying situations that would seem on the surface to preclude such rationality. While this may only indicate the protean nature of the concept of "economic rationality," it is a viable response. Similarly the apparent market failures can be dismissed either as nonexistent or as causing minimal economic loss. Harberger's earlier work[15] examines the question for the problem of monopoly power, and his chapter in this book presents a similar view critical of claims of inappropriate factor proportions in production. If such problems do not exist, then it is apparent that the policy of laissez faire continues to be viable and indeed desirable from a development standpoint. Once again the problem of development will be solved with the passage of time as the underdeveloped countries pass through the same stages as did the now developed countries.

On the other hand, it is admitted that there may indeed be deviations from laissez faire. The best example of this is the role which government has come to play in Third World countries. Government interferes in all areas, setting prices by nonmarket considerations, distorting the operation of labor markets through minimum-wage legislation and through providing employment in the government sector. In addition, the government artificially stimulates demand through deficit spending, thereby generating inflation in the domestic economy. In this case, the detrimental aspects cannot be overlooked; action must be taken. Government interference must be curtailed and the size of government deficits must be cut drastically. The best example of such an attempt is the effort to implement a "social market economy" in Chile after the military coup in 1973. This was seen as necessary because of the distortions caused to the economy by the previous socialist regime. Following the dictates of economic policymakers, generally trained at the University of Chicago, the government is attempting to implement the above policies, in essence moving the economy back to a market-based operation.

The planning response is quite different. Those with this perspective conclude that government must intervene in the economy to offset the antidevelopment impact of the two types of obstacles to development. On the side of nonrational behavior, the government can attempt to convince its citizens of the need for "modernization" while at the same time substituting its own entrepreneurial ability and knowledge to fill that vacuum. On the side of markets, the government can again offset the difficulties through economic planning. By developing a coherent overview of the economy and by forcing this on the actors in the economy through the various means at its disposal, the orthodox result of growth in income can be attained.

It should be pointed out here that the willingness of government to begin to supplement or supplant the market has another important result. It also opens the door to a deviation from consumer sovereignty in deciding the availability of goods to the economy and brings to the fore questions about the distribution of income which are generally submerged in the laissez faire approach. These questions can no longer be ignored because it is obvious in a planned economy that income distribution is highly conditioned by the political process, not given by some endowment of ability and drive. This suggests that the problem of the "social-welfare function" must be taken into consideration, and the definition of development must be consciously decided rather than simply taken as growth in output.

The preponderance of work in the orthodox mold can fit into either of the two responses noted above. We must now take note of the recent work of the "growth-with-

equity" group which is a response to the historical record
of development programs in the postwar period.

The Growth-with-Equity Response

While there are important differences between the laissez
faire theorists and the planners, they both agree in their as-
sessment of the success of postwar development. They both
point to the resounding success of the effort to raise growth
rates of GNP. As Morawetz[16] points out, "GNP per capita
of the developing countries grew at an average rate of 3.4%
per annum during 1950–75, or 3.0% if the People's Republic
of China is excluded. This was faster than either the developed or the developing nations had grown in any comparable period prior to 1950, and exceeded both official goals
and private expectations." While there is diversity in GNP
performance across countries, there is an almost universal
increase in other indicators of welfare such as life expectancy, which has increased as much in the past two decades
in developing countries as it did in a century in the industrialized nations.[17] The same can be said about the tremendous increase in the availability of education and about performance on measures of literacy.[18] Of course, these data
take into account both the socialist and the capitalist countries, and thus the success cannot be ascribed solely to the
advance of capitalism. But the capitalist countries have succeeded in these terms, which seems to indicate the success
of the orthodox strategy.

Despite its success in raising growth rates of GNP, the
orthodox strategy of economic development has seemingly
failed in some crucial areas: there is continued unemployment, increased income inequality within and among nations, and the stagnation of real income levels among the
poorest. The common theme that animates all of these
criticisms is that the benefits of the orthodox strategy of
development have failed to "trickle down" to the poor of

the world, and thus there must be a new strategy, growth with equity. Let us look at these failures more closely.

In employment, the general experience has been that unemployment has risen despite the high growth rates; it exists in the world today on an enormous scale, much more severe than in the 1930s. Some economists argue that open unemployment in the world is going up at the rate of 8 percent a year, though Morawetz is much less alarmed. Of note is that this widespread unemployment emerged during the 1960s, a decade of worldwide expansion of trade and rapid growth in the economies of developed countries, and that it often appeared in the countries that were growing the most rapidly.

The second change that is apparent in the data is an increase in the inequality of income distribution in underdeveloped countries. While there is an active debate on the meaning of the data, since 1965 the share of Brazil's national income going to the top 5 percent of the people has risen from 29 percent to 38 percent, and by some estimates to 46 percent. In Kenya, the top 20 percent appears to receive 68 percent of the income; in Ecuador, 74 percent of the income; and in Turkey, 61 percent of the income.

The third problem area is absolute poverty: the inability of persons to provide for their basic needs. Adelman and Morris studied income shares in 43 noncommunist, underdeveloped countries during the post–World War II period.[19] They found that as economic growth proceeded, the share of the bottom 60 percent of the people fell relatively. But they also found that in poorer countries the income of the bottom 40 percent had fallen absolutely as well, i.e., these people had less income in absolute terms at the end of these two decades of development than they had had in the beginning. Adelman and Morris's statistical results correspond well with evidence gathered in certain areas: India, Pakistan, northern Mexico.

In response to these depressing results many orthodox

development economists began to search for ways to mod-ify their vision of "development=growth in per capita GNP" to include a concern for channeling the benefits of growth to the poorest. Thus there is emerging a third major response within the orthodox paradigm, one that has been termed "growth with equity."[20]

The growth-oriented theory of economic development stresses that inequality of income is necessary to provide incentives for investment. If self-interested, maximizing in-dividuals are allowed to seek differential rewards for their efforts and risk-taking, total income will be maximized in the process. Then (if you are a conservative) the benefits will eventually "trickle down" to the less successful in the form of higher wages; or (if you are a liberal) the state could redistribute the benefits when society is rich enough so that incentives will not be drastically impaired. Unfor-tunately, as seen above, the results of these two strategies in underdeveloped countries are not very encouraging. Forty percent of the people live and die all too early in the meantime.

The growth-with-equity adherents argue that the "grow now, trickle later" approach not only has problems of exe-cution but is badly flawed in its conception of strategy. Three problems are cited most commonly.

First, a country cannot grow now and redistribute in-come later because of the structures which develop with unequal growth. For example, as growth proceeds, those receiving the income obtain increased political power to oppose any attempt to redistribute later. In addition, in-come becomes embodied in goods—Mercedeses, luxury apartments, college educations—which cannot be redis-tributed. There is no way to turn a Mercedes into bicycles or a luxury apartment into public housing. Thus income becomes a stock which cannot be redistributed.

A second problem with the growth strategy is that the poor moved into the cities in far greater numbers than

theory assumed. Todaro[21] argues that for every job opening up in the cities, three people migrate from rural areas
looking for jobs. Thus, for every job created, two people
are attracted who end up unemployed. In addition, the
demonstration effect of urban life has been a major mag-
net in drawing people from the rural sectors to the urban
areas.

Finally the argument is made that certain key aspects of
the development process simply have been ignored. Agriculture is one of these. It was given the role of fueling the industrialization process by providing various surpluses. But
it turns out that this was often at the expense of the vital-
ity of the sector, and in many cases agriculture has become
unable to provide the basic food needs of the population.
Similar benign neglect was accorded broader social and political aspects of development, with little concern given to
social and political mobilization and participation.

Growth-with-equity economists are relatively united in
their critique of the economic growth strategy and there
are other areas of basic agreement as well. They generally
accept the idea that social revolution is unlikely and probably undesirable for most poor countries in the near future.
Thus these theorists are struggling to come up with an approach that will achieve some degree of equity short of
social revolution. They are convinced that the poor can
improve their standard of living without revolution, and
they cite Taiwan, Hong Kong, Israel, Japan, Singapore, and
Sri Lanka as examples of countries where this has happened.
This places them to some degree in the "history = progress"
school, but they are much less sure of this than of other orthodox responses.

Another common factor is their implicit assumption concerning the peasants in less developed countries. They regard most people in the poor countries as responsive to
economic opportunities; thus the bottleneck in the poor
countries is not the peasant, but is more likely the capital

city's powerful elite who have failed to design projects that provide meaningful opportunities to peasants. Common explanations of this failure are: first, the people at the top do not understand the people at the local level and their needs; second, they have been following a development-from-above syndrome, keeping all the incentives, all the management, all the cash in the hands of the central planners; or, finally, they have been following misguided policies favoring urban consumers. Any effort at growth with equity must correct these inadequate economic policies.

Finally, growth-with-equity theorists all give considerable emphasis to the social and political variables in achieving growth and equity. They argue that one of the crucial limitations of past approaches was their narrow focus on simple economic factors—land, labor, and capital—to the exclusion of political, social, and cultural factors.

Despite these common starting points, growth-with-equity theorists espouse a wide variety of development strategies; in fact, some seven growth-with-equity strategies are discernible: employment generation, the redirecting of investment, the meeting of basic needs, human resource development, agriculture-first development, integrated rural development, and the New International Economic Order.[22] They are not all mutually exclusive, of course, and some are quite complementary. They simply approach the problem of eliminating poverty from different angles. Their unifying thread is the intention to deliver greater benefits to the bottom half of the population.

The two most fundamental strategies are "meeting basic needs"[23] and the "New International Economic Order."[24] In this book, Paul Streeten focuses on the former and Celso Furtado on the latter. Streeten argues that the goal or target of development should be to meet the basic needs of all people everywhere—food, water, clothing, shelter, medical care, education, and participation in decisionmaking. In addition to meeting these needs directly, employment

generation,[25] the redirection of investment,[26] human resource development,[27] agriculture-first development,[28] and
integrated rural development[29] can all be seen as indirect
ways of meeting basic needs.

All but one of these strategies focus on efforts within the
underdeveloped countries. However, those who call for a
New International Economic Order argue that while internal
changes are necessary they cannot succeed without a major
restructuring of those international institutions—the international monetary system, tariffs, multinational corporations, etc.—that at present result in discrimination against
the poor countries.

It should be noted that growth with equity has not
brought unanimity to the orthodox camp. The tradition-
alists within the orthodox paradigm retort that the growth-
with-equity case is built on sand. They claim that the data
are insufficient to prove a worsening of living standards and,
in addition, that traditional strategies are being judged too
soon. Western development exhibited increasing unemployment and income inequality as a stage before growth finally
spread its benefits to the poorest part of the population.
More time is needed before the growth approach can be declared a failure.

While the growth-with-equity approach developed within
the orthodox paradigm and still has one foot firmly planted
there, its tendency to endorse policies that supplant markets
and deliver goods and services directly begins to move it
closer to the political-economy paradigm. Certainly many
of those who call for a New International Economic Order
are adherents of dependency theory, one of the two main
variants of the political-economy paradigm. Celso Furtado
is one of the best examples.

At this point the boundaries between the two paradigms
become blurred, and the view of history as progress is not
so clear. The growth of unemployment, inequality, and absolute poverty certainly have tarnished that belief. We

will return to these questions after consideration of the political-economy paradigm.

IV. The Political-Economy Paradigm

The other main approach to development is what we term the political-economy paradigm. It takes a very different stance from the orthodox approach, and the contrast highlights the arena of paradigm competition.

Within the orthodox paradigm the more traditional laissez faire and planning economists focus on economic growth as the key to development, while the growth-with-equity economists concentrate on the distribution of the benefits of growth to the poor. Political economists are more concerned with the *nature of the process* by which economic growth is achieved.[30] In addition, traditional economists look on people's values as means. Since the goal is growth, if people's values have to change in order to get growth, then society must effect that change. But for political economists, one goal is to enhance people's core values. Development becomes the means, not the end, for the end is to enhance what people value. Development or growth is desirable only if it is consistent with people's deepest values. Thus, political economists such as Denis Goulet define development as "liberation."[31]

This means liberation from oppressive and exploitative relationships both internally, among people within the country, and externally, among nations. The key question is: Who is controlling the development process? To apply Paulo Freire's terminology of the educational process[32] to the development process implies the question: Are people (or classes) and nations *objects* of development under someone else's control or are they *subjects* of development, in control of their own destiny?

Development is thus seen as the unfolding, in human

history, of the progressive emancipation of peoples and nations from the control of nature and from the control of other peoples and nations. A major task then becomes that of explaining why this process has progressed much more with some peoples and nations than others. At this point there emerge within the political-economy paradigm two major schools of thought—the Marxists and the dependency theorists. The key difference between them resides in where they identify the locus of power and control. The control and use of the economic surplus of society is seen as the key to power and control of development. The Marxists focus on the internal class structure as the key to understanding control of the economic surplus. Dependency theorists focus on relationships between nations. This is primarily a matter of emphasis. Marxists have always been concerned with imperialism, and dependency theorists are concerned with the connection between the internal class structure and external dependency. But the different emphasis is important in understanding the political-economy paradigm.

The economic or social surplus is viewed as a residual factor—that which remains after necessary consumption has been subtracted from total output. Political economists argue that control of this economic surplus determines the nature of the development process. If a landed aristocracy controls the surplus you will get one style of development, if the middle class controls it then you will get a different style. The degree of foreign control of the surplus also will shape the strategy of development.

The economic-surplus concept is used by both Marxists and dependency theorists to analyze historical development and explain the existence of underdevelopment. We now turn to that analysis.

Development and Underdevelopment

At least at a superficial level, the stance of the political economist vis-à-vis history is quite similar to that of the orthodox writer. As Marx said, "the developed countries simply show the less developed countries their future." Thus the forces of nature will of necessity push economies from a precapitalist stage through the capitalist stage into either a socialist stage, which is the prelude to a communist society for the Marxist, or into self-reliance within a New International Economic Order for the dependency theorist. The process is inexorable, ensuring that history will bring progress. Nonetheless, there is a substantial difference between the two paradigms on specifics of the process. Whereas an automatic process was simply assumed by the orthodox approach, no such automatic transit is assumed by the political economists. The progress of history will come about only through the efforts of men: "Man makes himself." It will be through a long and costly struggle that history will advance, with each phase containing within it contradictions which must be exploited and which in their resolution will move the system the next step on the path. But those who control the economic surplus at a given time will not give in easily and thus progress will always be difficult. But it will come about as history and development move synchronously.

In this paradigm, the theory of underdevelopment has received the bulk of the interest, for it is only by understanding the forces of underdevelopment that the contradictions can be located and the struggle launched to resolve them. Let us take as our starting point the treatment of Western capitalist development, common to both variants of the political-economy paradigm, which, in turn, is the springboard for their separate theories of underdevelopment.

Capitalist Development in Europe and the United States

The development of capitalism in the West faced the need for change in the social structure so that the change-oriented middle class could become the leaders of society. This often involved a more or less violent struggle for supremacy between the old social order and the emerging new one. The English Revolution of 1640, ending with the supremacy of Parliament in 1688, replaced the feudal lords with the landed gentry and urban middle class as the dominant classes in England, thus preparing the way for later economic progress. The Frech Revolution of 1789 replaced the old aristocracy with the new middle class. The lack of such social change was a major factor in the economic stagnation of Spain after the seventeenth century.

This change in social structure enabled the economic surplus to be productively used. As Professor Dudley Dillard has pointed out: "Productive use of the 'social surplus' was the special virtue that enabled capitalism to outstrip all prior economic systems. Instead of building pyramids and cathedrals, those in command of the social surplus chose to invest in ships, warehouses, raw materials, finished goods and other material forms of wealth. The social surplus was thus converted into enlarged productive capacity."[33]

Before this productive investment could take place, the economic surplus had to be channeled into the hands of the new progressive class of society. In England, the profit inflation (the rise of money prices faster than rents and/or money wages) of 1540–1640 and 1795–1815 redistributed income in the first instance from landlords with fixed money rents to the rising gentry and merchants, and in the second from wage earners to profits on capitalist enterprise. Also the lag of real wages behind increases of productivity in the eighteenth and nineteenth centuries further increased profits from which new investment was made. This accumulation of capital enabled new technology to be utilized, which, by reducing costs, enabled more capital to be accumulated.

Such a period of development is always characterized by discontent and unrest because of the great changes taking

place. In the case of the development of the capitalist countries, this required action on the part of a powerful national
state to facilitate the social changes and accumulation of
capital and to suppress any attempted interference with the
process.

The appearance of a new "spirit" not only facilitated social change in the capitalist countries but also promoted capital accumulation and economic development. The Protes-
tant ethic encouraged thrift and reinvestment of savings by
the middle classes, and hard work and obedience by the
working classes.

The sum of these historical events was a social revolution
that destroyed the old feudal social order and brought to the
fore a new class that was change oriented, and into whose
hands the economic surplus was channeled for productive
use. This, coupled with the rationalization of agriculture
that took place, enabled capital to accumulate and economic
development to proceed.

Since this process revolutionized the economies of Western Europe and North America, why did it fail to do so in
Asia, Africa, and Latin America? That is, what are the causes
of underdevelopment suggested by the two political economy
variants?

Two Theories of Underdevelopment

Let us start with the Marxist view. Capitalism entered
most underdeveloped countries the "Prussian way"—not
through the growth of small, competitive enterprise but
through the transfer abroad of advanced large-scale business. Thus, capitalist development in these countries has
not been accompanied by the rise of a strong property-
owning middle class and by the overthrow of landlord domination of society. Rather, an accommodation has taken
place between the newly arrived business class and the socially and politically entrenched agrarian aristocracy.[34]

Therefore, there is neither vigorous competition between enterprises striving for increased output and rationalized production, nor accumulation of the economic surplus in the hands of entrepreneurs forced by the competitive system and the spirit of a middle class society to reinvest as much as possible in the continuous expansion and modernization of their businesses. The result is that production is well below the potential level, with agriculture still being operated on a semifeudal basis, and with waste and irrationality in industry protected by monopoly, high tariffs, and other devices.

For these and other reasons the actual economic surplus is much lower than the potential social surplus, which is the difference between the output that could be produced in a given natural and technological environment and what might be regarded as necessary consumption. A large share of the potential social surplus is used by aristocratic landlords in excess consumption and the maintenance of unproductive laborers. In addition, a large share of the actual social surplus is taken by businessmen for commercial operations promising large and quick profits, or for the accumulation of investments or bank accounts abroad as a hedge against domestic social and political hazards. Furthermore, in order to obtain social status and the benefits and privileges necessary for the operation of a business, they must emulate the dominant aristocracy in its mode of living. The potential social surplus is further reduced by the substantial quantity of resources used to maintain elaborate and inefficient bureaucratic and military establishments.

Although other factors undoubtedly have much to do with the inadequacy of the amount and composition of investment, the waste of a large portion of the social surplus due to the prevailing social structure is probably one of the major causes of economic stagnation.

In addition, the prevailing social and economic structure breeds a system of social relations, habits, customs, and culture that retards social and economic development. The preindustrial attitudes of peasants and workers operate against change, but even more important is the attitude of the ruling classes and the state which they usually dominate. These ruling classes know that if social and economic development comes, their power, status, and way of life will be threatened. Therefore, they continuously and actively oppose all kinds of social change.

The governments of these countries are poor agencies for enforcing the necessary changes, even though they claim the desire to do so, because often they are controlled or at least heavily influenced by these same wealthy classes. Governments which have attempted basic alterations in the social and economic structure have usually fallen, victims of a coup d'etat.

Many of these governments fear the prospects of development; their ruling classes realize better than we do the revolutionary potential which is contained in social change. They realize that even an attempt at peaceful, evolutionary development could quickly gain momentum and proceed to a situation where whole social classes are destroyed and basic institutions remolded.

John Gurley has elsewhere encapsulated this view quite succinctly:

> Social scientists these days usually suppose that all governments really want economic development, and if they do not achieve it, then it must be because the problems are unusually difficult to solve, or that solutions take a rather long time to work themselves out. Persistence and technical knowledge are what is required for success. This supposition, however, does not adequately take account of the class structure of societies, the often conflicting aims that exist among the various classes, and the class nature of "success" and "failure." When poverty is looked at from the standpoint of the ruling classes, it may not be a failure of the system at all but rather a pre-

requisite for the continuation of their accumulation of wealth, their privileges, and their social, political, and economic domination of the society. . . .

A thorough-going programme of economic development, which is spread widely and reaches deeply into the structure of the society, is a dangerous thing to ruling classes, for it tends to undermine the very attributes of the masses of people that nourish the wealthy and powerful. Such a programme awakens people, and it is often best that they doze; it mobilizes people for gigantic economic efforts and such organization can be turned into political subversion; it sweeps away illusions, but may open their eyes to the causes of their own oppression.

Furthermore, any serious economic development programme that involves industrialization threatens existing class structures by creating new economic bases from which arise new social classes, and weakens the economic foundations which support the present dominant classes.[35]

Thus there is little likelihood that underdeveloped countries will simply progress along the path which has been traversed before. Capitalism has failed in its historic mission to develop the Third World. Rather, they are doomed to underdevelopment unless they undertake a process of struggle to take advantage of the contradictions of the capitalist order.

Dependency theorists would not necessarily disagree with this view of Third World underdevelopment; but they would argue that it does not give enough emphasis to the underdeveloped countries' own history and to their interaction with the developed countries.

Starting with the historical studies of underdevelopment pioneered by Celso Furtado, André Gunder Frank, Keith Griffin, Osvaldo Sunkel, and others, a dependency perspective on this process of development and underdevelopment has been in the making, particularly in regard to Latin

America. This structural approach builds on the history of capitalist development presented above. The development of capitalism and the world market is seen as a twofold process. A highly dualistic *process of underdevelopment* of Africa, Asia, and Latin America is the consequence of the *process of development* of Europe and North America. This twofold process created a situation of dependence in which the underdeveloped countries became appendages of the developed countries.

This approach emphasizes the role of dependence in shaping the internal economic, social, and political structures (and thus control of the economic surplus) and in shaping the external relations of underdeveloped countries. Dependency means that many of the most important decisions about development strategies—decisions about prices, investment patterns, government macroeconomic policies, etc.—are made by individuals, firms, and institutions external to the country.

The simplest way to understand the meaning of underdevelopment in dependency theory is to see it as a process whereby an underdeveloped country, characterized by subsistence agriculture and domestic production, progressively becomes integrated as a dependency into the world market through trade or investment. Its production becomes geared to the demands of the world market and particularly of the developed countries, with a consequent lack of integration between the parts of the domestic economy. Thus both agriculture and industry become export oriented.

Two Views of Development

The final component of the models is their theory of development. Here the lack of elaboration is as notable as the wealth of analysis in the theory of underdevelopment. The Marxist theory of development suggests that the capitalist structures which exist and inhibit the development of Third

World countries must be overthrown and replaced by a socialist society. This will in turn become a communist society over time, but the basic step must be the overthrow, violent or otherwise, of the capitalist structures.

What is to be done after the revolution? Political economists, Marxists, and dependency theorists alike have not developed any *theories* of development. Rather Marxists and many dependency theorists have drawn empirical generalizations from the historical development experience of the Soviet Union and China. Until recently the Soviet model of development was looked to for guidance in development strategies. Thus it is worthwhile to take a closer look at it.

The Soviet model,[36] as historically derived, can be subdivided into three aspects: the preconditions of the model, the institutions characteristic of the model, and the strategy of development in the model.

The preconditions of the model include severance of any existing colonial bond with capitalist countries, elimination of economic domination by foreign capitalists, and redistribution of political and economic power. In sum, this will usually mean a social revolution which, at least nominally, redistributes political and economic power to the workers and peasants.

The institutions characteristic of the model include collectivized agriculture, publicly owned enterprises, comprehensive central planning, centralized distribution of essential materials and capital goods, and a system of administrative controls and pressures on enterprises, in addition to incentives, to ensure compliance with the plan.

The strategy of development in the model encompasses high rates of capital formation; priority of basic capital goods industries; bias in favor of modern, capital-intensive technologies in key processes combined with labor-intensive techniques in auxiliary operations; an import-substitution policy in international trade; utilization of underemployed agricultural labor for capital formation; and heavy investment in human capital.

Parallel, in time and intent, to the revolt of the growth-with-equity theorists within the orthodox paradigm, many Marxists and dependency theorists turned to Chinese experience as an alternative to the Soviet model of development. Many factors played a role in this shift in allegiance: the Soviet obsession with growth that relegated people's values to a secondary position, the concentration of power in the hands of the Communist party at the expense of the mass of people, the focus on industrialization to the neglect of agriculture, and so on.

To many political economists China seems a more appropriate model of development.[37] A great deal of work has been done on the accomplishments in China. A review of this literature finds extensive and numerous treatments of China's gains in health care, sanitation, worker organization in industry, rural development, and rural mobilization. It is apparent that if China had not existed, political economists would have had to invent it, for the validation that it gives to the political-economy approach is substantial and crucial.

The general model drawn from Chinese experience is one in which self-reliant development is pursued with an emphasis on fulfilling people's basic human needs (food, shelter, health, education) and on providing institutional structures (brigades, communes, etc.) that enable people to exert control over the conditions in which they lead their lives. John Gurley's chapter in this volume elaborates many of the specific lessons to be gleaned from Chinese experience.

Most dependency theorists are more circumspect about citing China as their model of development. They concentrate instead on the elimination of dependency relations through the call for a New International Economic Order. This is frequently coupled with a rather vague endorsement of a self-reliant socialism that is without the dictatorial political control of China. Thus, their major concern is returning control of the development process to the individual nation-states. Some dependency theorists realize that eliminating external dependency does not necessarily empower the mass of poor people in the underdeveloped countries. A class analysis demonstrates that the leading elites in many underdeveloped countries—particularly those countries most integrated into the international economy— are less than eager to pass control to the poor.[38]

In general, then, political economists see the historical process of development sidetracked into the blind alley of underdevelopment. Traditional Marxists see this as due to the failure of the middle class to perform its historical mission of creating a dynamic capitalist society. Dependency theorists argue that specific conditions led to a dependent relationship between center and periphery countries that distorted the development of the latter. Marxists call for social revolution to replace the middle class with control by workers and peasants, and dependency theorists call for an end to dependency so nation-states can take control of their own development.

In closing this discussion of the political-economy paradigm it should be noted that this reading of historical development is not universally agreed upon by political economists. As Gurley points out, writers such as Bill Warren, although speaking from a Marxist perspective, claim that there have been tremendous increases in the forces of production in the postwar period, that development is indeed occurring in exactly the way that Marx would have predicted. Countries such as Brazil, Mexico, and Nigeria are going through a capitalist revolution. This process and its success will bring forth the contradictions which will eventually lead to a socialist overthrow of the capitalist system. Thus, these political economists agree with the traditional economists of the orthodox paradigm that development is occurring. They differ in believing that, after development occurs, conflict that will eventually lead to socialist revolutions will develop among all the advanced capitalist countries. Here again, the boundaries between the two paradigms become blurred, but these two sections should have made clear the basic utility of the paradigm division.

Nonetheless, it is the contention of the remainder of this chapter that it is necessary to pass beyond these paradigms and, in particular, to break free of their implicit belief in the natural progress of history. We suggest that seeing history as "convoluted" avoids many of the reductionist failings of our postwar paradigms, and in general that the remaining chapters of the volume should be taken as examples of analyses which do move beyond these confines.

V. Convoluted History

Let us turn initially to the remaining chapters and their relation to the paradigm framework. As will be seen from an initial reading, the chapters seem to correspond directly to the paradigms. The essay by Arnold Harberger is squarely in the orthodox paradigm. From the empirical information which he uses, he draws the important conclusion that factor markets seem to be working, and adjustments of input proportions, as a result of relative factor price differences, seem to be taking place. Thus, in this topical area the expectations of a market view of the development process are apparently borne out by the data. The essay on basic needs by Paul Streeten certainly falls into the growth-with-equity version of the orthodox paradigm.

Similarly, John Gurley and Celso Furtado seem to fit nicely within the political-economy paradigm. Gurley, the Marxist, has a dialectical view of history and takes a much broader view of development and its processes, noting always the central role of class structure and conflict. Furtado comes from the dependency school, and his development of that theory again places him outside of the orthodox view and into a context which is much more in tune with the political-economy paradigm. All in all, the essays obviously fit fairly well with the paradigm construct.

But a closer examination indicates that there are some differences. This is most apparent in the essay by Gurley; but to Furtado and Streeten as well, the world appears as a much more complex affair than adoption of a particular paradigm would seem to permit. We would like to suggest that these thinkers have been forced to supersede the paradigm division in their attempt to evaluate the phenomena of development from an objective perspective and that they have been able to draw upon what is valuable on either side of the debate. This step has become necessary because a confrontation with the concrete reality of particular countries at specific times clearly shows that strict adherence to the paradigms obfuscates rather than illuminates. Contemporary examples abound.

A look at the postwar record indicates that countries prospered and stagnated regardless of social system or development strategy. Brazil and Mexico grew while their poor suffered. Costa Rica grew and Cuba failed to grow while their poor prospered. Both China and Taiwan are cited as "models" of development. Both Tanzania and Peru are floundering. Capitalism has not brought freedom to Chile or South Korea and socialism has not brought liberation to Cambodia or North Korea. There have been increases in both per capita GNP and malnutrition, decreases in both infant mortality and political freedoms, and decreases in both external dependency and control by the poor of their own lives. This concrete record of "progress" challenges us to rethink our approach to "development."

As noted above, the starting point for thinking about

development is some conception of history. An initial response to our idea of convoluted reality which might aid in understanding the later chapters would be to become wary of the accepted conception of history and to attempt to avoid assuming the view of historical progress which is common to both of the paradigms. History as we live it simply does not seem to be moving in that direction. The parable of historical progress common to both the orthodox and political-economy paradigms is a metaphor that may be useful in studying an abstraction— civilization or socialism—but it is misplaced in studying the actual development of Peru or Uganda.

Nisbet' summarizes the difficulty succinctly and elegantly:

> The relevance and utility of the metaphor of growth are in direct proportion to the cognitive distance of the subject to which the metaphor is applied. The larger, more distant or more abstract the subject, the greater the utility of metaphor-derived attributes. . . .
>
> We may now state the proposition in reverse. The less the cognitive distance, the less the relevance and utility of the metaphor. In other words, the more concrete, empirical and behavioral our subject matter, the less the applicability to it of the theory of development and its several conceptual elements.
>
> It is tempting enough to apply these elements to the constructed entities which abound in Western social thought: to civilization as a whole, to mankind, to total society; to such entities as capitalism, democracy, and culture; to social systems as functionalists and others conceive them; and to so-called evolutionary universals. Having endowed one or other of these with life through the familiar process of reification, it is but a short step to further endowment with growth—with internal mechanisms of growth and development around which laws of progress and evolution are constructed. Such has in very large measure been the history of

social thought in the West since the time of Aristotle.

It is something else entirely, however, when we try, as much social theory at present is trying, to impose these concepts of developmentalism upon, *not* constructed entities, but the kind of subject matter that has become basic in the social sciences today: *the social behavior of human beings in specific areas and within finite limits of time.* Efforts to extract this further from the metaphor of growth are . . . wholly unsuccessful.[39]

Convoluted History, Convoluted Development

It might be well to examine an alternative view of history, one which comes out of the writings of the Latin American novelist, Gabriel García Márquez. In his major work, *One Hundred Years of Solitude,*[40] García Márquez provides us with a parable of Latin American history since independence which is quite at variance with our progress notion. History moves forward, progresses, but it is always doubling back upon itself. In some cases the march of history gets mixed up and only later resumes its "natural" course. This view we can call "convoluted history."

Let us briefly review the story of the book to aid our understanding. It is the history of a village, Macondo, from its founding to its demise, as seen though the eyes and lives of one family, the Buendías. Ostensibly there is the progress which we call development. From an obscure, virtually deserted swamp Macondo grows and its people prosper. Macondo experiences technical or scientific progress as new inventions become known: ice, the astrolabe, the pianola. It experiences economic progress as the diversity of activities increases, the capstone being the arrival of a banana company which raises per capita GNP substantially. It also experiences political modernization as the national political structure develops and incorporates Macondo into its bosom.

Throughout these experiences of progress, there are doubts. The inventions of science, known for years elsewhere, are used by the gypsies to dominate the people of Macondo. The banana company effects substantial changes in the town and the people; but when the company cannot have its own way, it leaves town and calls down a tremendous rain which "purifies" the town of its past. In addition, the political structure is often quite repressive and unresponsive.

But the real questioning of historical progress comes·from viewing the lives of the Buendías. Every generation has two recurring tendencies. One is the "Aurelio" tendency, calm and reflective, given to studying the historical manuscript of the family, yet when challenged, able to react with fury. In one case the fury was so great as to drive Colonel Aurelio to lead thirty-two unsuccessful rebellions.

The other recurring tendency is the "José Arcadio" tendency. This describes modernizers, the entrepreneurs, who participate and enjoy the new changes which history is bringing them, and usually die a violent death. But history is more complex than simply continuity and repetition. For at one point the twins, Aureliano Segundo and José Arcadio Segundo, are mixed up; and they live part of their lives acting as the other. Finally history triumphs and brings them back to their own nature.

But underlying the currents of history is one consistent concern: the attempt to understand and to decipher the parchments left by Melquiades the gypsy. There is a gradually growing understanding, which reaches its fruition when the last Aureliano, Babilonia, learns to read the parchments which are the entire history of his family condensed into one moment. As he reads, that history ends and is blown away by the wind "because races condemned to one hundred years of solitude did not have a second opportunity on earth."

This is certainly a different version of history.

Yet it is a version which may fit the process of development better than the idea of "progress," and it is one which can place the chapters of this book in a useful perspective. In some sense the writers of the later chapters are attempting to decipher the parchments of development, to read and understand the history of development in Third World countries. In addition, they are doing so in an effort to wipe out that history, to call forth the wind to banish underdevelopment and to facilitate policy which can bring about meaningful development.

The import of García Márquez's parable of convoluted history is that there is no simple historical march of progress. There are no general paths to development just as there is no general definition of development. Each people must write its own history. As Denis Goulet says regarding the strategy of development pursued by Guinea-Bissau: "Paradoxically, the lesson of greatest importance is that *the best model of development is the one that any society forges for itself on the anvil of its own specific conditions.*"[41]

What does this mean for the development economist? There is an interesting parallel in modern medicine in a tension between the "scientific" explanation of a disease and the diagnosis a clinician makes for a particular patient.[42] This is well described by Tolstoy in *War and Peace*:

> Doctors came to see Natasha, both separately and in consultation. They said a great deal in French, German and in Latin. They criticised one another, and prescribed the most diverse remedies for all the diseases they were familiar with. But it never occurred to one of them to make the simple reflection that they could not understand the disease from which Natasha was suffering, as no single disease can be fully understood in a living person; for every living person has his complaints unknown to medicine—not a disease of the lungs, of the kidneys, of the skin, of the heart, and so on, as described in medical books, but a disease that consists of one out of the innumerable combinations of ailments of those organs.

While Tolstoy's depiction of every illness as a unique event may no longer be justified, economic development is even more of an art than medical diagnosis. Economic theorists can scientifically explain the results of underpricing capital regardless of country or time. Development economists, on the other hand, are diagnosticians of the particular illnesses of particular countries at specific points in time. They are forced to transcend a specific scientific paradigm to become artisans of the particular. It is in this way that the essays in this volume extend and transcend their paradigms and thus truly advance our knowledge of development.

The Later Chapters

As we look at the following chapters we see an interweaving of views, a mixing of the paradigms, as history crosses on itself. While the authors might disagree on the evidence presented by Harberger in support of the orthodox paradigm, all would agree to the importance of the phenomenon which he treats and of the results he obtains. They are less likely to adopt the belief that each people, if let alone, will adapt to their environment efficiently, generating an increase in per capita GNP. But the result obtained by Harberger will not be dismissed by any of them.

The basic-needs approach represented in the chapter by Paul Streeten draws upon components of both paradigms, and, as a result, it has received criticisms from both sides. Critics within the orthodox paradigm consider a basic-needs approach inefficient, unfeasible, and an ideological concept that conceals a call to revolution. Critics from the political-economy paradigm argue that local elites will oppose the program or use it to forestall a needed social revolution. But these criticisms are deduced from general theories, not analyses of particular cases. As

Streeten says, "It is evident that a wide variety of political regimes have satisfied basic needs within a relatively short time." Streeten makes the case for striking out and seeking an alternative of growth with equity through new approaches to development tailored to the particular situation of each country. A basic-needs approach must draw upon the best from both the orthodox and political-economy paradigms and combine it with the uniqueness of individual underdeveloped countries if it is to be anything other than rhetoric. Each country must design its own system for delivering basic needs.

In his essay, Celso Furtado, a major contributor to the development of dependency analysis, transcends the confines of that approach. This is seen most clearly in his formulation of much of the international problem as being the ability to deal with an "age of global reconstruction." In other words, although many of the actors are the same—the nation-states, the international organizations, the transnational corporations—the historical epoch in which all are participating is fundamentally different from the earlier period which saw the development of dependency theory. In dealing with these differences and with their implications for both center and periphery countries Furtado makes his major contribution. His is an optimistic view, seeing the subordination of economic criteria to social values and a convergence to a new conception of development as part of a new effort at civilization, where each of the peoples of the world will write its own history, a history which is not one of unilinear progress but which is convoluted and unique.

This melding of paradigms in confrontation with history is nowhere clearer than in the chapter by John Gurley. He clearly breaks out of the confines of the Marxist paradigm and begins to weave the complexity of history, pointing out the successes that have been obtained by countries in each of the two or three camps, while not slighting their failures. Thus, the Aurelianos and the José Arcadios, our temporizers and our modernizers, are mixed between the camps. While Gurley still feels that the socialist countries have performed better, it is important to understand the environmental or genetic factors which may have led to the failures of particular socialist countries or the successes of particular capitalist countries. Even the definitions of capitalism and socialism are transformed. This is parchment reading of the best sort.

This throwing off of the conceptual blinders of the paradigms holds out hope that development will become a means to serve people and that there will be fewer tragedies like Chile and Cambodia, where people are seen as a means to promote development. "If there is to be a possibility of choosing a human path so that all human beings may become the active subjects of their own history, it must begin at the level of new analysis. . . . Development should be a *struggle* to create criteria, goals, and means for self-liberation from misery, inequity, and dependency in all forms. Crucially, it should be the process a people choose, which heals them from historical trauma, and enables them to achieve a newness on their own terms."[43]

We hope that this book will contribute to that struggle.

NOTES

1. Thomas Kuhn, *The Structure of Scientific Revolution*, 2nd ed. (Chicago: University of Chicago Press, 1970).

2. W. W. Rostow, *The Stages of Economic Growth: A Non-Communist Manifesto* (New York: Cambridge University Press, 1960).

3. P. Bauer and B. Yamey, *The Economics of Underdeveloped Countries* (New York: Cambridge University Press, 1967), p. 151.

4. B. Higgins, *Economic Development: Problems, Principles and Policies* (New York: W. W. Norton, 1968), p. 147.

5. D. Seers, "The Meaning of Development," in Charles K. Wilber, *The Political Economy of Development and Underdevelopment* (New York: Random House, 1973), p. 6.

6. Denis Goulet, " 'Development' . . . or Liberation," in Wilber, *Political Economy*, p. 355.

7. Furtado also points out how development and progress have come to be focused on the nation-state as the major operational entity. In our treatment we will take as an unexamined premise that the basic unit of analysis is the nation-state. Gurley's essay indicates the empirical validity of this approach even with reference to the socialst states which place "internationalism" on a very high plane.

8. J. Culbertson, *Economic Development: An Ecological Approach* (New York: Alfred A. Knopf, 1971).

9. See J. H. Boeke, *Economics and Economic Policy in Dual Societies* (New York: Institute of Pacific Relations, 1953) and Higgins, *Economic Development*, chap. 12, "Cultural Determinism."

10. See David C. McClelland, *The Achieving Society* (Princeton, N. J.: D. Van Nostrand, 1961).

11. See David E. Novack and Robert Lekachman, eds., *Development and Society: The Dynamics of Economic Change* (New York: St. Martins, 1964), "Part Two: The Social Order"; Bert F. Hoselitz, *Sociological Aspects of Economic Growth* (New York: Free Press, 1960); Everett E. Hagen, *The Economics of Development*, rev. ed. (Homewood, Ill.: Richard D. Irwin, 1975), chap. 11, "Entrepreneurship."

12. See Ragnar Nurkse, *Problems of Capital Formation in Underdeveloped Countries* (Oxford: Basil Blackwell, 1958). See also the relevant chapters in Higgins, *Economic Development*, and Hagen, *Economics of Development*.

13. See particularly Bauer and Yamey, *Economics of Underdeveloped Countries*.

14. See Hagen, *Economics of Development*; Higgins, *Economic Development*; Culbertson, *Economic Development*; and a host of other works.

15. A. Harberger, "Using the Resources at Hand More Effectively," *American Economic Review*, May 1959.

16. D. Morawetz, "Twenty-Five Years of Economic Development," *Finance and Development*, September 1977, p. 10.

17. Ibid., p. 12.

18. Ibid., p. 13.

19. I. Adelman and C. Morris, *Economic Growth and Social Equity in Developing Countries* (Stanford: Stanford University Press, 1973).

20. See James H. Weaver, Kenneth P. Jameson, and Richard N. Blue, "Growth and Equity: Can They Be Happy Together?" *International Development Review*, 1978/1, pp. 20–27, reprinted in Charles K. Wilber, ed., *The Political Economy of Development and*

40   Paradigms of Economic Development

Underdevelopment, 2nd ed. (New York: Random House 1978).
Also see Mary Evelyn Jegen and Charles K. Wilber, eds., *Growth
with Equity: Essays in Economic Development* (New York: Paulist
Press, 1979).

21. Michael P. Todaro, "A Model of Labor Migration and Urban
Unemployment in Less Developed Countries," *American Economic
Review*, March, 1969, pp. 138–148.

22. This is based on Weaver, Jameson, and Blue, "Growth and
Equity . . ."

23. In addition to the essay by Paul Streeten in this volume, see
Overseas Development Council, *The United States and World Development: Agenda 1977* (New York: Praeger, 1977).

24. See the following: Mahbub ul Haq, *The Third World and the
International Economic Order*, Overseas Development Council, De-
velopment Paper 22, (September 1976); Guy F. Erb and Valeriana
Kallab, eds., *Beyond Dependency: The Developing World Speaks
Out* (Washington, D.C.: Overseas Development Council, 1975);
Antony J. Dolman and Jan van Ettinger, eds., *Partners in Tomorrow:
Strategies for a New International Order* (New York: E. P. Dutton,
1978).

25. See International Labour Office, *Employment, Growth and
Basic Needs: A One-World Problem* (New York: Praeger, 1977);
Kenneth P. Jameson and Charles K. Wilber, "Employment, Basic
Human Needs, and Economic Development," in Jegen and Wilber,
Growth with Equity.

26. See Hollis Chenery, et al., *Redistribution with Growth* (Oxford:
Oxford University Press, 1974).

27. See Irma Adelman, "Growth, Income Distribution, and Equity
Oriented Development Strategies," *World Development*, February-
March, 1975; reprinted in Wilber, *Political Economy*, 2nd ed.

28. See John Mellor, *The New Economics of Growth* (Ithaca:
Cornell University Press, 1976).

29. See Albert Waterson, "A Viable Model for Rural Development," *Finance and Development*, December 1974 and March 1975;
reprinted in Wilber, *Political Economy*, 2nd ed.

30. For a full discussion of alternative definitions of development
see Peter J. Henriot, "Development Alternatives: Problems, Strategies,
Values," in Wilber, *Political Economy*, 2nd ed.

31. See Goulet, " 'Development' . . . or Liberation," in Wilber,
Political Economy, 2nd ed.

32. See Paulo Freire, *Pedagogy of the Oppressed* (New York:
Herder and Herder, 1970). Chapter 1 is reprinted in Wilber, *Political
Economy*, 2nd ed.

33. Dudley Dillard, s.v. "Capitalism" *Encyclopedia Britannica*
(1963); reprinted in Wilber, *Political Economy*, 2nd ed.

34. See Paul A. Baran, "On the Political Economy of Backwardness," in Wilber, *Political Economy*, 2nd ed. Celso Furtado, a dependency theorist, has a similar analysis. See Celso Furtado, *Diagnosis of
the Brazilian Crisis* (Berkeley: University of California Press, 1965),
pp. 20–21, 115–118.

35. John Gurley, "Rural Development in China 1949–72, and the
Lessons to Be Learned from It," *World Development*, July–August
1975, p. 456.

36. For a full treatment see Charles K. Wilber, *The Soviet Model
and Underdeveloped Countries* (Chapel Hill: University of North
Carolina Press, 1969).

37. For the classic statement of the Chinese model see John Gurley,
"Maoist Economic Development: The New Man in the New China," in
Wilber, *Political Economy*, 2nd ed.

38. Fernando Henrique Cardoso and Enzo Faletto, *Dependencia y
Desarrollo en América Latina* (Santiago: ILPES, 1967).

39. Robert A. Nisbet, *Social Change and History: Aspects of the
Western Theory of Development* (New York: Oxford University
Press, 1969), pp. 267–268.

40. Gabriel García Márquez, *One Hundred Years of Solitude* (New
York: Harper and Row, 1970).

41. Denis Goulet, *Looking at Guinea-Bissau: A New Nation's
Development Strategy*, Occasional Paper no. 9: Overseas Development Council, March 1978, p. 52.

42. The following is based on the discussion of a related issue taken
from Stanley Hauerwas, David Burrell, and Richard Bondi, *Truthful-
ness and Tragedy: A Further Investigation in Christian Ethics*, "An
Alternative Pattern for Rationality in Ethics" (Notre Dame, In.:
Notre Dame Press, 1977).

43. James J. Lamb, "The Third World and the Development
Debate," *IDOC-North America*, January–February 1973, p. 20.

Perspectives on Capital and Technology in Less-Developed Countries

Arnold C. Harberger*

I. Introduction

As AN OUTGROWTH of more than two decades of work in and observation of less-developed economies (principally in Latin America and Asia), I feel that I have learned a number of lessons that I would like to share with my professional colleagues. Some of the lessons are substantive, and two of them constitute the two major parts of this article. The first of these has to do with the fact that there is little tendency for rates of return to capital (either social or private) to be higher in the less-developed countries of the world than they are in the major industrial centers. The second lesson is that there is no truth in the notion that the less-developed countries are condemned by modern technology to use (in their more modern sectors) capital and labor in proportions that are very similar

*I would like to express my gratitude to the National Science Foundation for financial support of the research, reported herein. I would also like to thank Luis Alvaro Donoso and Victor Levy for help going far beyond the duties normally assigned to research assistants. An early version of this paper was presented as the annual Frank W. Paish Lecture at the 1977 meeting of the (United Kingdom) Association of University Teachers of Economics. Copyright © 1978 Arnold C. Harberger.

to those employed in the advanced economies. These are the substantive lessons. But there are also lessons at another level which (depending upon one's taste) might conceivably be called methodology but might alternatively be classified as relating to the spirit with which research on LDC economies is conducted. This lesson builds on a recognition that the data of LDCs are limited both in quantity and quality. Gaps exist in time series; the concepts underlying data sets change unexpectedly from time to time; and one never knows up to what point one can put faith in the actual numbers one sees. These facts of life have, singly and in combination, managed to sap the enthusiasm of many young scholars who have ventured with initial high hopes into the area of research on developing countries. I think this is unfortunate, because much can be done with data that are quite imperfect. Gaps can be bridged by the use of artful assumptions on interpolation; missing figures can be estimated on the basis of knowledge of other economies; and finally, the results of particular empirical exercises can be tested for their sensitivity to particular types of bias that might systematically affect the data being used. In what follows, there is something of each of these solutions to the data problems mentioned above. And the lesson that emerges is, I think, a reasonably hopeful one. To my mind, at least, the data problems of LDCs are better regarded as a fascinating challenge than as a dispiriting roadblock standing in the way of the advancement of our scientific knowledge.

The first major problem is the measurement and comparison of rates of return to capital across countries. In this article the measurement is effected using a methodology which is common across the countries studied. This introduces comparability (at least at a certain level) in the resulting figures. It also provides a way of checking the plausibility of particular assumptions, arbitrary in themselves, that have to be made along the way and, at the same time, it makes possible scientific tests for the errors that may be involved in such assumptions (by seeing how different the final results of the exercises would be if one had used the actual data of a country known to have reasonably reliable figures in place of the arbitrary assumptions actually made). Needless to say, I would not be speaking in these tones if I did not feel that only small errors were introduced by the use of the particular arbitrary assumptions employed in this study.

The main calculations underlying the estimation of rates of return to capital are reviewed in sections II and III. Section II deals with the measurement of the capital stock; section III with that of the income attributable to capital (the numerator of the rate-of-return ratio). In section IV the results of these calculations are put together to form rates of return and the latter are then employed to test alternative hypotheses. In section V some sensitivity tests are applied to check the robustness of the results.

Sections VI and VII deal with the second of the substantive lessons mentioned at the outset. In section VI, a methodology is devised for deriving a "predicted" level of employment of labor, per dollar of gross return to capital in a particular industry i and country j. These "predictions" are based on the assumption (hypothesis) that factor proportions in the industry in question must be the same in country j as in a particular country of comparison (in this case the United States). Using the methodology developed in section VI, statistical tests are made in section VII of various hypotheses concerning relative factor proportions between the United States on the one hand and the LDCs on the other. In this experiment, the basic data are 727 different ratios of "predicted" to "actual" labor usage in different three-digit industries scattered across some eighteen LDCs. Viewing these 727 observations as a sample drawn from a much larger population (many more industries, many more countries) of such ratios, we test hypotheses concerning what the underlying population from which the sample of 727 was taken might look like. The conclusion is very strong that the data are quite consistent with the notion that the median three-digit industry in the modern sector of the typical LDC uses something like four times the amount of labor that would be predicted on the basis of United States factor proportions. The data are equally strong, moreover, in rejecting the notion that this population median can be as low as 3.5 times, let alone 3.0 times the United States figure.

II. Measuring the Stock of Reproducible Capital

The measurement of capital stock is surely the most straightforward aspect of our calculations. All of our calculations were based on national accounts data (indeed, in the final analysis, our choice of countries with which to work was largely determined by the ease with which their national accounts data could be fitted into our methodology). All of the countries in question had investment broken down into components. We chose to work with only three components—buildings, machinery and equipment, and inventories. For some countries our procedure entailed our aggregating, say, their series of housing investment with their series on investment in business plants so as to produce a series on investment in buildings. Needless to say, the national accounts data that we worked with were those expressed in real terms. Thus we are not faced with the problem of finding the relevant price deflators. The basic methodology that we used was a perpetual inventory technique, applied separately to the three investment categories. In this procedure, we used arbitrary rates to reflect how time and use erode the real economic value of the assets in question.

For buildings we assumed depreciation at the rate of 2.5 percent per year; for machinery and equipment the corresponding figure was 8 percent per year. For inventories we obviously did not need a depreciation rate, as the national accounts investment figures already expressed inventory investment as the net change in stock.

The missing link at this point is an estimate of the capital stock of each of the three types of assets at some initial or base year. This, happily, was a problem that I had faced before,[1] with reasonable success. The trick in this case is to find in the past some span of a few years (say, three) during which one judges that the economy was operating in reasonably "normal" circumstances. The critical dimension in which "normality" is important is that the capital stock of the different types should be growing at the same rate as the GNP. We then take the gross investment figures, say, for machinery and equipment in these three years (say, 1955–57), and average them so as to reduce the impact of random variation. The resulting average investment we treat as if it were the investment of 1956, the middle year. The normal function of gross investment is to replace depreciating capital and to provide for the growth of the stock. The equation

$$I_t = (\delta + \gamma)K_{t-1}$$

is a familiar way of expressing this fact. Our trick, then, was to use the average investment of three years as a center estimate of I_t in the above equation. The depreciation rate, δ, was simply the one assumed for the category (.08 in the case of machinery and equipment) and the rate of growth, γ, was simply the average rate of growth of the country's GNP over the three-year period (here 1955–57) in question. Thus, if I_t would have averaged 140 over the 1955–57 period, and if GNP had grown at the rate of 6 percent over that same period, then we would have estimated the end-of-1955 capital stock of machinery and equipment at 1,000 $[- 140/(.08 + .06)]$.

This type of exercise was performed for all the countries in the study. The base years differed, depending on how far back the relevant national accounts series could be obtained, but in any case a base-year figure was estimated for each category in each country. It is quite clear that this procedure is much less restrictive than assuming that, over the entire period of observation, the marginal capital-output ratio is equal to the corresponding average ratio. This latter assumption is particularly dangerous in countries whose growth rates change dramatically over time. Usually capital accumulation is only one of many factors, and probably not the most important one, in causing an abrupt acceleration or deceleration of the rate of growth. The assumption that marginal and average ratios are the same imputes to capital accumulation an incredible importance (omnipotence) in the growth process. I am confident, therefore, that we are correct in avoiding the use of marginal capital-output ratios as a device for working back to capital stock figures, at least so far as the capital stock for buildings and for machinery and equipment is concerned.

I have fewer qualms about using a somewhat similar procedure in the case of inventories, however; for, frankly, I tend to see the accumulation of inventories as something which follows the growth process, not something that causes it. Certainly I do not think that there is anything immutable about the ratio of inventories to GNP, but the assumption of a rough proportionality over the ranges of variation that we have observed during the past ten to twenty years does not appear to me to be one that will lead to gross error in the final figure for global capital stock. Thus it is that initial inventories were estimated by dividing the accumulated investment in inventory over the period of observation (say, 1956 through 1975) by the increase in GNP from 1955–75. The resulting ratio—a 20 years' accumulation of inventories divided by a 20-year change in GNP—would then be our estimate of the inventory/GNP ratio. Applying this to 1955 GNP we would obtain our estimate of the 1955 level of inventories.

Using the methodology just described, it is relatively easy to go the rest of the way and derive capital stock series for each of the three types of investment goods, year by year from the initial base period until the most recent year for which data are available. This is what was done. The methodology was the same from country to country, with the exception of the choice of base year. This choice, however, does not have any systematic influence on the figure for, say, the 1970 or 1971 capital stock of a country. What we must recognize is simply that the capital stock estimates are likely to be more accurate the farther in the past is the base year that was used. This is because, if the base year is twenty years back, much of the initial capital stock estimated for that year will have in the interim been depreciated away. The capital stock for 1970 or 1971 will accordingly be relatively insensitive to errors in estimating an initial capital stock as far back as 1952. However, if the base year is 1965, much less of the base-year stock will have been depreciated away by 1970 or 1971, and accordingly our estimate of capital stock for these latter years would be more influenced by any error that might be involved in a 1965 estimate of base-year stock.

Note that up to this point no mention has been made of land. Yet land presents problems that must be faced in any estimation of rates of return to capital based on national accounts data. The problem is that the investment figures in the national accounts cover reproducible capital only, while the income figures in the national accounts include income accruing both to reproducible capital and to land. Hence he who seeks to estimate rates of return on the basis of national accounts data must make his choice. He may either:

(a) build up an estimate of reproducible stock in the way we have outlined in this section, then add to it an independently obtained estimate of the value of land, and finally derive a rate of return using this global capital stock as the denominator, with the numerator being the total net income assigned in the national accounts to profits, interests, rents, etc.; or

(b) estimate only the reproducible capital stock along the lines indicated above, and estimate a rate of return on it by taking out of the numerator a portion of income deemed to be attributable to land.

In the exercises being reported, the second of these two procedures was followed.[2] Thus we have no need to estimate the value of land as such, though we must find some way of separating out the income attributable to reproducible capital from that attributable to land. The methods used to achieve this end are reported in the next section.

We have so far described the procedures for estimating a country's total stock of reproducible capital. For some purposes, however (such as measuring a private rate of return), a measure of the privately held stock is required. To obtain this stock measurement we separated each year's investment into the parts effectuated by the public and private sectors. The most common problem that arose in the course of this exercise was that figures were available for total public investment but were not discriminated by type. In such cases it was assumed that the shares of "machinery and equipment" and of "inventory investment" in total public investment were equal to half of the corresponding shares (as shown in the aggregate data) for total investment. This assumption obviously implies that the share of construction in public-sector investment was larger than that for private investment.

The procedure just described was used to generate a breakdown of public-sector investment into the three categories here employed (construction, machinery and equipment, and inventories) for all those countries for which such a breakdown was not directly available. Once so discriminated, public-sector investment of each type was subtracted from the corresponding total investment figure in order to obtain private investment by type. Finally, the annual data on private investment by type were treated in a fashion identical to that described above for total investment, so as to generate (by a perpetual inventory technique) annual estimates of private capital stock by type of asset.

III. Measuring the Income from Reproducible Capital

In many LDCs, the national income accounts are broken down by final product classification (consumer durables, consumer nondurables, investment in buildings, investment in machinery and equipment, etc.) and by an industrial classification of value added (agriculture, manufacturing, communications, services, etc.) but not by type of income (wages, salaries, interest, rents, profits) accruing to the ultimate recipients. Such countries had automatically to be excluded from the present study, since the methodology used here for analysis requires data on national income by type.

But even among countries whose national accounts contain the appropriate classification, some difficulties still remain. Principal among these is the fact that, though most income types are easily assignable to either labor or (physical) capital, each country has one category, usually labeled "income from unincorporated enterprises" or something closely akin to that, which quite obviously includes, apart from the return to capital, some income that should properly be imputed to the labor of the proprietors and their families.

Various methods have been employed to break the "income from unincorporated enterprises" aggregate into a part assignable to family labor and a part assignable to capital. The most common method is to evaluate the labor of proprietors and their families on the basis of the average wages paid to hired labor in the industry in question. Another is to add to the income of unincorporated enterprises the wages paid by them to hired labor, and the interest and rents paid by them for "hired capital," to obtain a "national income originating in unincorporated enterprises in a given industry or sector." This "national income originating" is then assumed to be divided between labor and capital according to some principle or rule, such as the assumption that the shares of labor and capital in the unincorporated part of an industry or sector are the same as those applying in the corporate part (for which the relevant data are easier to come by).

Unfortunately, methods like those just listed have massive data requirements. Moreover, their application is likely to give rise in particular cases to special problems (for example, an imputed labor income that systematically exceeds the total reported income of unincorporated enterprises), which then would have to be resolved on an ad hoc basis. Considerations such as these helped motivate our decision to solve the problem by imputing to labor a specified constant fraction of the income from unincorporated enterprises (or its counterpart category) in each of the countries we examined. The fraction chosen for the present study was one-half, which lies at the center of a plausible range from perhaps one-third to something like two-thirds. Sensitivity tests can then be applied to see to what extent (if any) the principal conclusions of the study are affected if the assumed fraction is varied within this range (for individual countries or for the group as a whole).

A similar procedure was used to impute the income accruing to land. Here the assumption was made that pure land rent was equal to one-third of that national income originating in agriculture, plus one-tenth of the rental value of dwellings. Once again, these should be regarded as rough orders of magnitude, with the final estimates emerging from the exercise being subject to sensitivity tests.

In measuring the income from capital, care must be taken to be explicit about the underlying concept that one is trying to approximate. Here we have taken two alternative concepts. The first attempts to measure the marginal net productivity of capital. As such it is defined to be net of depreciation but gross of all taxes. Thus such items as corporation income taxes and property taxes are included in the income from capital. In addition, indirect business taxes such as sales taxes, value added taxes, stamp taxes, sumptuary excise taxes, etc., must be considered. Our procedures assign the yield of these taxes to capital and to labor in proportion to their contributions to gross national product, building on the principle that excise taxes are equivalent to a set of equiproportional taxes on all elements of cost (including allowances for depreciation). In our exercises, this assignment is done on an aggregate level, but there is no doubt that it would be preferable to do the job in a disaggregated way, tax by tax and industry by industry.

The second concept of return to capital is a "market rate of return." As such it is net of all taxes except the personal income tax, on the presumption that the market rate tends to be equalized across different sectors and types of capital, while the rates of return after personal tax will be different for different taxpayers, even on identical investments. In what follows we shall refer to the market rate of return as a "private after-tax rate of return." This is simply to emphasize that it is not a measure of productivity or of social yield; it is a private rate of return in the sense of being net of all taxes that are paid before capital owners get their reward. It is not net of income taxes which are, in concept at least, paid after that reward has been received by the ultimate owners.

To measure the income accruing to private-sector capital we must eliminate not only the taxes just indicated but also whatever income accrues to capital in the public sector. Here again the necessary data were not always available in the desired form. In some countries' accounts the data given on the property income of government do not include the earnings of industrial enterprises in which the government is the principal or sole shareholder. In these countries, such enterprises are treated as autonomous and amalgamated with the private sector. Property income of government may include dividends actually paid out by these enterprises and received by the treasury, but it does not include their profits as such.

Our procedure in handling this difficulty is as follows. Where we could piece together, from different sources, estimates of the income from public enterprises as well as investments in them, we defined the public sector broadly, including investments in public sector enterprises as additions to the public sector's capital stock and simultaneously counting the full profits of public-sector enterprises as part of the income from capital of that sector.

On the other hand, where the available data gave us only investment in the government sector—the buildings, parks, roads, vehicles, etc., built and/or owned and used by the various ministries and agencies—we sequestered these figures out of the total capital stock and took from the earnings of capital only such profits as may have been generated in the government sector, thus narrowly defined.

The column showing private after-tax rates of return

therefore varies in its precise meaning from country to country. In all cases some part of the total income from capital has been taken out of the numerator of the aggregate national rate of return, and some part of the total capital stock has been taken out of its denominator. However, in some cases that part has been narrowly defined to be that corresponding to the government sector, while in others it was defined more broadly so as to include all public sector enterprises. Where the data permitted a choice, we opted for the broad definition; but in all cases the definition of the public sector used in dealing with the capital stock was followed in defining the portion of income to be sequestered in the process of deriving the return to private-sector capital.

IV. Rates of Return and Factor Proportions

Once the results of the calculations outlined in the preceding sections have been obtained, it is an easy step to compute the relevant rates of return. For the present study, it was decided to work with data that were averages of three years (1969, 1970, and 1971) to moderate the influence of transitory factors. For each country, therefore, the ratios of income from capital to beginning-of-year capital stock were taken for 1969, 1970, and 1971. These ratios were then averaged to obtain the rates of return shown in Table 1.

It is notable how modest are the differences between the rates of return of the more advanced countries on the one hand and the LDCs on the other. The average national aggregate rate of return of the richest seven countries was 6.7 percent; that of the poorest seven was 8.4 percent. If Korea (a clear outlier) is excluded from the latter group, their average rate of return falls to 7.1 percent. Note that

TABLE 1

REAL RATES OF RETURN TO CAPITAL, 1969-71

Country	National Aggregate Rate of Return	Private After-tax Rate of Return
United States	0.085	0.076
Sweden	0.044	0.031
Canada	0.084	0.064
Germany	0.071	0.056
Belgium	0.079	0.058
Finland	0.057	0.048
United Kingdom	0.050	0.044
Greece	0.100	0.059
Argentina	0.098	0.106
Panama	0.065	0.039
Jamaica	0.108	0.094
Portugal	0.055	0.057
Costa Rica	0.057	0.048
Colombia	0.078	0.089
Honduras	0.065	0.077
Korea	0.163	0.152
Thailand	0.073	0.102
Sri Lanka	0.097	0.068

Sources: Based on national accounts data given in the United Nations *National Accounts Yearbook* and in publications of the World Bank, the OECD, and the Statistical Yearbooks of each country, and using capital stock figures generated from National Accounts Investment Series.

the 8.4 percent average for the poorest seven is just about equal to those for the United States and Canada, and that the 7.1 percent rate obtained by excluding Korea is equaled or exceeded by Germany and Belgium as well as by the United States and Canada.

With respect to the private after-tax rate of return the results are similar. The richest seven countries had an average real private rate of return of 5.4 percent; the poorest six (excluding Korea) had an average rate of 7.3 percent which compares with a rate of 7.6 percent for the United States.

These findings immediately bring to mind the question whether relative factor endowments have much to do with the rate of return that capital yields in different places. To inquire into this question we fitted regressions in which the rate of return to capital was the dependent variable and the capital-labor ratio the independent variable. For this purpose we would have liked to make a careful adjustment of the data on labor force for each country so as to define labor in terms of units of more or less constant quality. Various possible quality corrections were explored, such as constructing indexes in which workers with different educational levels were given different quality weights, but the data requirements of such corrections proved insurmountable. In the end, we settled for a rough quality measure calibrated to the per capita income of the countries. Taking unity as a central value for a quality index, Sri Lanka was assigned an index of 0.5 and Sweden one of 1.5. The quality indices for the remaining countries were then interpolated between these two, on the basis of the logarithm of their per capita income.

The results of this exercise are shown in the first two columns of Table 2. There it is seen that the adjusted labor force of Sri Lanka is 2,209 thousand, exactly half of the 4,418 thousand given for the actual number of workers. Similarly, the adjusted figure for Sweden is 5,119 thousand, or 50 percent more than the actual number of workers (3,413 thousand). Costa Rica, Portugal, and Jamaica are close to the point where the interpolated quality index is equal to unity.

The meaning of this adjustment is as follows: If a representative sample of the Sri Lanka labor force were to go to Sweden (and somehow surmount linguistic and cultural barriers), those workers should be able to earn an average

income equal to one-third that of the average Swedish
workers. If a similarly representative sample of the Costa
Rican labor force were to appear in Sweden, those workers
should be able to earn an average income equal to two-
thirds of the Swedish average. I leave it to each reader to
decide how apt he considers this choice of a quality cali-
bration. Certainly I have no basis to argue that it is the
"right" one, only that it is probably not very far wrong.
For example, I would think it absurd that a representative
sample of workers from Sri Lanka could earn in Sweden
no more than one-sixth of the average Swedish wage, and
equally absurd that they could earn as much as two-thirds
of the Swedish average. Likewise, I would be very surprised if a representative sample of Costa Rican workers
could not earn in Sweden more than half the Swedish average, and equally surprised if they could earn as much
as 80 percent of it. Thus, while the particular weights assigned for Sri Lanka and Costa Rica (relative to Sweden)
are admittedly not "accurate," they are certainly toward
the center of a plausible range. When similar hypothetical
exercises are carried out for the other countries on the
list, they lead me to a similar conclusion. Thus I suggest
that the quality correction made here should be broadly
acceptable as yielding the very rough sort of approximation that it was intended to give.

Tables 3 and 4 present the results of regressions in
which the independent variable is the amount of capital
per adjusted worker. Table 3 shows how insensitive is the
estimated rate of return to changes in K/L. On the other
hand the tight correlation between real wages and the ratio
of capital to adjusted labor is dramatic. When the relative
factor price (ρ/ω) is the dependent variable, the coefficient
is simply the sum of the coefficients of the two absolute
factor prices, but, interestingly, the correlation coefficients
for relative factor prices are lower than those for the real
wage rate.

TABLE 2

BASIC DATA FOR 1970

Country	Labor (thousands)	Adjusted Labor Force (thousands)	Capital Stock per Adjusted Worker (thousands of 1970 dollars)	Annual Earnings per Adjusted Worker (thousands of 1970 dollars)
United States	82,897	129,236	21.5	6.37
Sweden	3,413	5,119	20.3	4.84
Canada	8,813	13,193	17.8	4.50
Germany	26,610	37,893	12.0	3.26
Belgium	3,638	5,125	14.6	3.34
Finland	2,118	2,901	13.2	2.21
United Kingdom	25,715	34,715	9.6	2.86
Greece	3,235	3,872	6.1	1.89

Argentina	9,011	10,487	5.3	1.41
Panama	488	517	3.6	1.40
Jamaica	767	796	3.3	0.79
Portugal	3,395	3,490	2.8	1.33
Costa Rica	547	531	3.4	1.38
Colombia	6,225	5,273	3.1	0.72
Honduras	689	542	3.4	0.94
Korea	12,080	9,507	1.5	0.58
Thailand	16,850	11,562	0.9	0.33
Sri Lanka	4,418	2,209	1.3	0.94

Source: Labor force data from United Nations, *Demographic Yearbook*, 1970, supplemented where necessary by the statistical yearbooks of each country.

Note: Earnings and capital stock were converted into U.S. dollars using the average exchange rate for 1970 as given by the International Monetary Fund in *International Financial Statistics*. Where multiple rates prevailed, the principal trade rate was used.

TABLE 3

REGRESSIONS ON THE K/L RATIO

(Log dependent variable on log K/L)

Dependent Variable	Including Korea		Excluding Korea	
	Coefficient	R^2	Coefficient	R^2
National aggregate rate of return (ρ)	–0.116	0.128	–0.059	0.046
Private after-tax rate of return (r)	–0.214	0.281	–0.161	0.200
Earnings per adjusted worker (ω)	0.780	0.900	0.770	0.890
Relative factor prices (ρ/ω)	–0.897	0.822	–0.840	0.819

TABLE 4

PREDICTED RATES OF RETURN

Country	National Aggregate Rate of Return	Private After-tax Rate of Return
Canada	6.7	5.2
United Kingdom	7.0	5.7
Costa Rica	7.4	6.7
Sri Lanka	7.9	7.9
Range including predicted rates for 15 countries	6.7–7.5	5.0–6.9

The simplest hypothesis for explaining these findings is that there is an international capital market which tends to equalize rates of return to capital across countries in much the same manner as a national capital market tends to equalize rates of return across activities and regions. We certainly do not expect to observe that capital-intensive activities within a country have significantly lower rates of return than labor-intensive ones. The reason is that we presume that the various activities draw their funds from the same general capital market.

If, then, the capital market extends across national boundaries, as it surely does, should we not expect to find a similar (if perhaps somewhat weaker) tendency for equalization of yields to occur? Table 4 shows dramatically how little variation of yields is explained by variations in the K/L ratio. In fact, the regression values of the rate of return for fifteen countries lie between the limits of 6.5 to 7.5 percent for the aggregate rate of return and of 5.0 to 6.9 percent of the private after-tax rate of return. This indicates how little influence very strong differences in K/L ratios have in generating differences in the yield on capital. In sharp contrast to these results is the predictive power of the regressions for real wages and for *relative* factor rewards. Here the range of predicted values exceeds a factor of 10, and even the narrowest range including fifteen observations, spans a factor of more than 5.

The hypothesis explaining these results thus not only says that the rate of return to capital is brought to rough equalization through the international capital market, but also that the relative abundance or scarcity of labor (which does not move so readily across national boundaries) has a great deal to do with the determination of real wages.

V. Some Sensitivity Tests

In this section we first explore the sensitivity of the results with respect to the arbitrary assumptions made in the course of estimating the rates of return to capital. Later, we test for sensitivity to the possibility of a systematic understatement of capital investment.

Table 5 presents, for a sample of countries, the national aggregate rate of return as initially estimated. Then what that estimate would be if we had imputed to capital only one-third (rather than one-half) of the income from unincorporated enterprises. Finally, the third column shows how the results would be modified if we imputed to land a quarter rather than a third of agricultural GDP and 5 rather than 10 percent of dwelling rents.

As can be seen from the table, the basic pattern of rates of return does not change in any major way as one moves from column 1 to columns 2 and 3. If anything, column 2 exhibits a narrowing of the range of variation.

Our final sensitivity test concerns the possibility that investment may be systematically understated in the national accounts of most countries. Tax laws in particular give individuals and business firms strong incentives to carry out under the label of current expense acts that are in an economic sense acts of investment. Farmers digging irrigation canals, building fences, or planting orchards are unlikely to report these activities in such a way that they will be reflected as investment in the national accounts. Similarly, businessmen regularly make minor plant alterations or additions without reporting the sums concerned first as income, then as investment. What is actually classified as investment tends to be activity involving major construction projects on the one hand or the purchase of machinery and equipment whose function is too obvious to be disguised.

TABLE 5

NATIONAL AGGREGATE RATES OF RETURN

Country	As Estimated (1)	Imputing to Capital 1/3 of Income from Unincorporated Enterprises (2)	Imputing to Land 1/4 of Agricultural GDP plus 5 Percent of Dwelling Rent (3)
Sweden	0.044	0.039	0.046
Belgium	0.079	0.070	0.081
Finland	0.057	0.052	0.060
United Kingdom	0.050	0.045	0.051
Greece	0.100	0.070	0.106
Portugal	0.055	0.049	0.074
Thailand	0.073	0.045	0.074
Sri Lanka	0.097	0.069	0.111

To allow for the possibility of systematic understatement of investment in the national accounts of the various countries, we have recalculated the rates of return to capital on the assumption that the actual investment figures were 20 percent higher than the stated ones. This modification not only augments the capital-stock figures for any year by 20 percent, it also increases the income from capital by 20 percent of that year's stated net investment (the part that, by our hypothesis, was treated in the national accounts as a current expense rather than as an investment). Thus if $0.2 I_n$ represents more that 20 percent of the unadjusted income from capital, the numerator of the rate of return ratio will rise by more than 20 percent, and the rate of return itself will consequently rise as a result of the adjustment. Thus in Table 6, which presents the rate of return estimates resulting from this adjustment, some of the rates of return exceed, while others fall short of, their counterparts in Table 1.

Tables 7 and 8 replicate Tables 3 and 4, using the adjusted capital-stock and rate-of-return estimates. The principal conclusions remain unmodified. Regressions of rates of return on the capital-labor ratio fit poorly; regressions of real wages fit very well. Regressions with relative factor prices as the dependent variable also fit well, owing to the close relationship between real wages and the K/L ratio.

The regression values of the rate of return again fall in a narrow range (see Table 8), with fifteen countries falling within a range defined by a factor of 1.3 for the national aggregate rate of return and 1.4 for the private after-tax rate. By way of contrast, the narrowest range spanning fifteen regression values for relative factor prices is defined by a factor of 6.5 to 7.0, depending on which rate of return is used. The basic conclusion—relative insensitivity of the rate of return and strong sensitivity of real wages to relative factor endowments—thus remains unaltered if not reinforced as a consequence of the sensitivity tests.

TABLE 6

ADJUSTED REAL RATES OF RETURN

Country	National Aggregate Rate of Return	Private After-tax Rate of Return
United States	0.075	0.068
Sweden	0.043	0.042
Canada	0.078	0.061
Germany	0.070	0.057
Belgium	0.072	0.049
Finland	0.049	0.042
United Kingdom	0.048	0.041
Greece	0.085	0.062
Argentina	0.089	0.096
Panama	0.071	0.049
Jamaica	0.101	0.086
Portugal	0.059	0.061
Costa Rica	0.063	0.055
Colombia	0.074	0.083
Honduras	0.060	0.069
Korea	0.161	0.149
Thailand	0.099	0.093
Sri Lanka	0.092	0.062

Source: Capital stock figures and other data generated using 1.2 x National Accounts Investment Series.

VI. Methodology for Testing the Technology Hypothesis

In the present section we turn to the second substantive lesson mentioned in the introduction to this article. This concerns the degree to which LDCs are "condemned" to use technologies, invented in more advanced countries, which are (a) inappropriate to their factor endowments and (b) inflexible.

The approach we follow takes the U.S. Census of Manufactures as a base, and then predicts, industry by industry,

TABLE 7

REGRESSIONS ON THE $K*/L$ RATIO

Dependent Variable	Including Korea Coefficient	R^2	Excluding Korea Coefficient	R^2
National aggregate rate of return ($\rho*$)	−0.181	0.32	−0.131	0.25
Private after-tax rate of return ($r*$)	−0.206	0.36	−0.152	0.29
Earnings per adjusted worker (ω)	0.780	0.90	0.77	0.89
Relative factor prices ($\rho*/\omega$)	−0.966	0.87	−0.91	0.86

Note: Log dependent variable on log $K*/L$ is given, with data adjusted to incorporate the assumption that actual $I_t* = 1.2 \times$ stated I_t.

TABLE 8

PREDICTED RATES OF RETURN

Country	National Aggregate Rate of Return	Private After-tax Rate of Return
Canada	6.1	5.1
United Kingdom	6.7	5.7
Costa Rica	7.5	6.6
Sri Lanka	8.5	7.7
Range including predicted rates for 15 countries	5.9–7.6	5.0–6.8

the ratio of wage and salary payments to the gross earnings of capital for various LDCs. The comparisons are made for 68 three-digit industries, which were selected on the basis of two criteria: (1) they had to be industries for which there was a presumption that they would belong to the "modern" sector in an LDC (i.e., they could not include industries susceptible of including traditional handicraft activities), and (2) they had to be industries for which counterparts could be established between the United States industrial classification and that employed by the LDCs.

For each such industry the average wage paid was obtained by taking the ratio wage-and-salary payments as reported in the industrial census to the number of employed persons as reported in the same source. It was then assumed that if the same technological processes were employed in the LDC as in the United States for the same 3-digit industry, its wages bill (WN) per dollar of gross return to capital $(\rho_g K)$ would be equal to:

$$\left[\frac{W\hat{N}}{\rho_g K}\right]_{\text{LDC}} = \left[\frac{WN}{\rho_g K}\right]_{\text{US}} \times \frac{W_{\text{LDC}}}{W_{\text{US}}}$$

This assumes, in a sense, that the gross rate of return ρ_g is the same in the LDC as in the United States. The previous sections of this article lend credence to the view that rates of return in the LDCs tend to be close to those of the United States. If anything, it is likely that they may be slightly higher, in which case the prediction of LDC employment per dollar of capital return $(W\hat{N}/\rho_g K)_{\text{LDC}}$ would tend to be too high.

The next step is to compare the actual ratio of $(WN/\rho_g K)_{\text{LDC}}$ with the predicted one. This gives us, for each industry, the multiple by which actual employment exceeds that predicted by the constant-technology, no-substitution hypothesis.

The results of this exercise are presented in Table 9. Eighteen LDCs are represented in that table, and for each LDC the number of three-digit industries that were compared with their U.S. counterparts is given. Note that not all of

TABLE 9

DISTRIBUTIONS OF RATIOS OF ACTUAL TO "PREDICTED" LABOR PAYMENTS: 727 INDUSTRIES IN 18 LDC'S

Country	Number of Industries	First Quartile	Median	Third Quartile	Ninth Decile	Year
Singapore	32	5.0	6.5	9.1	15.6	1967
Argentina	40	1.5	2.1	3.1	8.0	1963
Venezuela	44	1.2	2.3	3.2	3.9	1963
Chile	43	4.5	7.4	11.9	19.8	1957
Mexico	41	1.7	2.1	3.2	6.9	1971
Costa Rica	34	1.1	1.6	3.0	3.9	1964
Peru	41	1.9	4.4	7.8	53.9	1963
Zambia	26	2.1	3.7	6.4	12.0	1972
Turkey	56	2.6	3.8	6.5	12.7	1964
Ecuador	41	3.4	5.8	13.8	19.8	1965
El Salvador	39	2.2	4.8	11.2	32.6	1961
Honduras	23	2.5	4.0	5.6	12.7	1966
Paraguay	36	1.4	3.3	9.9	40.3	1965
Korea	54	5.1	8.0	11.9	20.8	1967
Ghana	32	1.2	1.5	1.8	4.7	1967
Philippines	47	4.0	6.4	12.8	78.0	1961
Pakistan	49	3.1	4.5	7.0	19.6	1965
India	48	12.0	21.4	39.0	93.7	1966

Source: Industrial census (censuses of manufactures) of the listed countries. (Exchange rates used in the comparison of wages were those given by the International Monetary Fund in *International Financial Statistics* for the year in question. Where multiple rates prevailed, the principal trade rate was used.)

Note: "Predicted" payments are based on U.S. (1963) factor proportions plus actual wages in the given LDC industry.

the 68 U.S. industries had counterparts in any one of the LDCs. Note, too, that the dates of the industrial census used in the exercise vary from one LDC to another. These modest variations of date are not thought to impart any significant bias to the results. The hypothesis we are "testing" concerns the fundamental structure of industrial activity and employment in LDCs; this is not something which suffers dramatic changes over a year or a quinquennium.

In Table 9 an effort is made to convey, for each country, a sense of the distribution of the ratios of actual to predicted employment per dollar of return to capital. Toward this end, the third quartile observations are demarcated, as well as the ninth decile (that value which is exceeded by barely 10 percent of the observations).

VII. Discussion and Testing of the Results

It is clear from Table 9 that there are a great many three-digit industries in which relative factor use in the LDCs is found to be 5, 6, even 10 and 20 times as labor-intensive as in the United States. This should not be taken to suggest that these countries use very different machines than the United States, or that more workers operate a particular machine when it is running. We have not yet found a convenient way to have two typists simultaneously working at a given typewriter or two chauffeurs simultaneously driving a given car. That is simply not the way capital-labor substitution takes place.

It is more accurate to think that factors of production are employed with contingencies in mind. The guest-room furniture may be used only a few days per year, yet the family feels it is worthwhile to have it. The function of the telephone is in considerable measure simply to be there in the event a call comes in, or someone wants to make an outgoing call. Skiers find that if they do more than three or four days' skiing in a year, it pays to own the capital equipment (skis, boots, poles, etc.) rather than to rent it.

These homely examples are meant to put the reader in the right frame of mind to appreciate how capital-labor substitution really takes place as one moves from capital-rich to labor-abundant countries. In capital-rich countries it is worthwhile to have equipment around which may not be actually used very often, but which justifies its presence because it saves expensive man-hours. In labor-abundant countries, menial labor is so cheap that it often does not pay to buy labor-saving machines. Moreover, the differences in relative scarcity of menial versus highly qualified labor means that much saving of the latter takes place through the intensive use of the former. It is likely, for example, that the peons (runners) who sit outside executive offices in India can earn their meager daily pay simply by one or two errands for their boss. Their marginal productivity is measured in the value of the time they save their boss in running to get cigarettes, to buy a newspaper, to take a message down the hall.

These examples more aptly give the flavor of capital-labor substitution in LDCs than does the image of many workers piled up at a given machine, or even of any strong tendency to multiple-shift work (which is actually not much more prevalent in LDCs than in advanced countries).

As a final exercise, let us attempt to generalize, statistically, on the basis of the observations summarized in Table 9. For the present purpose, I would like to imagine those 727 observations as a sample drawn from a much larger universe of all possible comparisons between industry i in less-developed country j, and its counterpart in the United States.

Let the population of industry-country comparisons cover all modern industries (excluding again those which are traditional handicraft activities in the LDCs), and even all less-developed countries. Instead of 68 three-digit industries there might be 200 or more that fit these requirements, and instead of 18 LDCs we surely would have well over 100. So the universe from which our "sample" of 727 was drawn might be perhaps as large as 10,000 (recalling that not all industries are represented in a given LDC).

Thinking now about that universe, consider the variable in question to be the ratio of "predicted" to actual employment in industry i and LDC j, per dollar of gross return to capital. That variable obviously has some median value in the universe we are dealing with. Our hypotheses and our tests will deal with that median.

If that median were 4.0, what is the probability that a sample of 727 would contain as many as 51.9 percent (or as few as 48.1 percent) of observations in excess of 4.0? The answer is about a 30-percent probability. We therefore cannot plausibly reject the hypothesis that the true median is 4.0.

However, suppose the median of the universe were 3.5. What then would be the chance that a sample of 727 observations would have as high a percentage of observations in excess of (or below) the median as we observe in our sample? *That* probability is less than one in a thousand.

Finally, suppose the population median were 3.0. Then the chance of a sample of 727 yielding results as extreme as those we observe would be *less than one in a billion!*

These results are presented in Table 10. The conclusion, then, is that the typical LDC, if it is constrained by modern machinery at all, is put in a position where on the whole, in modern industrial activities, it uses on the average 4 times the amount of labor used in similar activities in the United States per dollar of return to capital. To say that that figure is as low as 3.5 or 3.0 is grossly inconsistent with the evidence. To pretend that, somehow, fixed proportions reign, industry by industry, across countries is erroneous beyond belief.

TABLE 10

TESTS OF HYPOTHESES CONCERNING FACTOR PROPORTIONS

Hypothesis: Median Factor Payments Ratio for all 3-digit LDC Industries is:	Proportion of 727 Sample Observations above Median Defined in Col. (1)	Probability (two-tailed) of an Occurrence as Extreme as (2) if Hypothesis of (1) were True
(1)	(2)	(3)
4.0	0.519	~.30
3.5	0.569	<.001
3.0	0.632	<.000000001

Note: Standard error of sample proportion $\sqrt{pq}/N$ = .0185.

NOTES

1. Arnold C. Harberger, "On Estimating the Rate of Return to Capital in Colombia," in *Project Evaluation* (London: Macmillan; and Chicago: Markham, 1972), chap. 6, pp. 132–156; and "Private and Social Rates of Return to Capital in Uruguay" (with Daniel Wisecarver), *Economic Development and Cultural Change* 25, no. 3 (April 1977): 411–445.

2. In my two previous attempts at estimation of this type, I took the opposite tack and tried to obtain independent estimates for land. I found this line of approach not only to require a great deal of search for adequate data, but also to be quite country-specific. That is to say, the ways of attacking the problem which seem most reasonable for Colombia were quite different from those that seemed best in the case of Uruguay. In the light of this I could not feel at all comfortable trying to impose a single uniform methodology for estimating the value of land across countries that were very different in nearly all relevant respects. I feel much more comfortable with the use of common procedures for attributing income to land. As will be seen, these procedures are flexible in the sense that they attribute more income to land in countries in which agriculture is more important, etc.

A Basic-Needs Approach
to Economic Development

Paul Streeten*

I. Basic Needs: Premises and Promises

Objectives

A BASIC-NEEDS APPROACH to development (BN) starts with the objective of providing the opportunities for the full physical, mental, and social development of the human personality and then derives ways of achieving this objective. It focuses on mobilizing *particular* resources for *particular* groups which are identified as deficient in certain resources (e.g., caloric adequacy by age, sex, and activity). It concentrates on the nature of what is provided rather than on income. It is therefore a more positive and concrete concept than the double negative of "eliminating poverty" or "reducing unemployment." It does not replace the more aggregate and abstract concepts, which remain essential to measurement and analysis; it gives them

*The views expressed are purely personal and not necessarily those of the World Bank. I am indebted for helpful comments to Shahid Javed Burki, Robert Cassen, Mahbub ul Haq, Richard Jolly, Frances Stewart, and T. N. Srinivasan. An earlier version of the first section of this article appeared in the *International Development Review* 19, no. 3 (1977) and of other parts in the *Journal of Policy Modeling*, March 1978.

73

content. Nor does it replace concepts that are means to broader ends, like productivity, production, and growth. From the idea of meeting basic human needs it derives the need for changing the composition of output, the rates of growth of different components, and the distribution of purchasing power.

In addition to the concrete specification of human needs, in contrast to (and in supplementation of) abstract concepts, and the emphasis on *ends*, in contrast to *means*, BN encompasses "nonmaterial" needs. Unlike the means to the satisfaction of some material needs, the means to the satisfaction of these needs, cannot be dispensed, but nonmaterial needs are a vital component of a BN approach, not only because they are valued in their own right, but also because they are important conditions for meeting material needs. They include the need for self-determination, self-reliance, political freedom and security, participation in making the decisions that affect workers and citizens, national and cultural identity, and a sense of purpose in life and work. While some of these nonmaterial needs are conditions for meeting the more material needs, there may be conflict between others, such as meeting basic material needs and having certain types of freedom. For other sets of needs, there may be neither complementarity nor conflict.[1]

Income Approach versus Basic Needs

The BN approach is contrasted with the income approach, which recommends measures that raise the real incomes of the poor by making them more productive, so that the purchasing power of their earnings (together with the yield of their subsistence production) is adequate to enable them to buy (and grow the produce of) the basic-needs basket. The BN approach regards the income orientation of earlier approaches as inefficient or partial, for seven reasons.

(1) There is some evidence that consumers are not always efficient optimizers, especially in nutrition and health, or when changing from being subsistence farmers to being cash earners. Additional cash income is sometimes spent on food of lower nutritional value than that consumed at lower levels (e.g., polished rice for coarse grains or rice for wheat) or on items other than food.

(2) The manner in which additional income is earned may affect nutrition adversely. Female employment may reduce breast feeding and therefore worsen the nutrition of babies, even though the mother's income has risen; or more profitable cash crops may replace "inferior" and "cheaper" crops grown and eaten at home, such as millet; or dairy farming, though employment-creating, may divert land from producing cheaper but more nutritious maize.

(3) There is maldistribution within households, as well as between households. Women and children tend to be neglected in favor of adult males. Both (1) and (2) raise difficult and controversial questions about free choice and society's right to intervene and about effective methods of aiding choice and strengthening and reaching the weak.

(4) Perhaps 20 percent of the destitute are sick, disabled, aged, or orphaned children; they may be members of households or they may not. Their needs have to be met through transfer payments or public services, since, by definition, they are incapable of earning. This group has been neglected by the income and productivity approach to poverty alleviation and employment creation. Of course, the existence of this group also raises particularly difficult problems of implementation, not only in poor societies.

(5) Some basic needs can be satisfied only, or most effectively, through public services (education, health,

water, sanitation), through subsidized goods and services, or through transfer payments. These services and those under (4) call for progressive taxation, indirect taxation of luxury goods, and for a system of checks against abuse. The provision of public services is not, of course, a distinct feature of BN. But the emphasis on investigating why public services have so often failed to reach the groups for whom they were intended, or were claimed to be intended, and insuring that they do is a feature of BN.

(6) The income approach has paid a good deal of attention to the choice of technique but has neglected to provide appropriate products. In many developing societies, the import or domestic production of oversophisticated products, which are transferred from relatively high-income, high-saving economies, has frustrated the pursuit of a BN approach by catering to the demands of a small section of the population or by preempting an excessive slice of the low incomes of the poor. The choice of appropriate products, produced by appropriate techniques, giving rise to more jobs and more even income distribution, which in turn generates the demand for these products, is an essential, distinct feature of the BN approach and is not necessarily fully achieved by a redistribution of income.

(7) Finally, as already mentioned, the income approach neglects the importance of nonmaterial needs, both in their own right and as instruments for meeting more effectively and at lower costs some of the material needs. This point becomes particularly relevant if the nonsatisfaction of nonmaterial needs (like participation) increases the difficulty of meeting basic needs more than the difficulty of achieving income growth.

The selective approach makes it possible to satisfy the basic human needs of the whole population at levels of income per head substantially below those that would be required by a less discriminating strategy of all-around income growth, and therefore sooner.

This point is crucial. If an unfortunate but apt metaphor is permitted, the choice is between precision bombing and devastation bombing. By attacking the evils of hunger, malnutrition, disease, and illiteracy with precision, their eradication (or at least amelioration) can be achieved with fewer resources (or sooner) than by choosing the roundabout road of raising incomes.

We may think of a gap between available resources and resources required to meet basic needs, though this way of putting it is somewhat mechanical because it neglects alternative methods of mobilizing these resources. The great merit of a BN approach is, then, that it can close this gap more successfully for two reasons: first, because it requires fewer resources for closing the gap in a given time (or the same resources can close it more quickly), and second, because it makes more resources *available*.

Fewer resources are *required*, or the objective can be achieved sooner, because a direct attack on deprivation economizes those resources on which income would be spent that do not contribute to meeting basic needs. These include, in addition to improvements in the effective instruments of implementation: (1) the non–basic-needs items in the consumption expenditure of the poor; (2) part of the non–incentive consumption expenditure of the better off; and (3) investment expenditure to the extent that its reduction does not detract from constructing the sustainable base for meeting basic needs.[2]

In addition, these fewer resources needed show a higher productivity in meeting basic needs. A combined operation for meeting an apppropriately selected package of basic needs (e.g., water, sewerage, nutrition, and health) economizes resources and improves the impact, because of linkages, complementarities, and interdependencies between different sectors.

Finally, a direct attack on infant mortality;[3] increased education for women; and even what is apparently the purest welfare component, the provision for old age, illness, and disability are thought to reduce desired family size and fertility rates more speedily and at lower costs than raising household incomes.[4] The causal nexus has not been established beyond controversy, but it is one of the hypotheses produced by the BN approach. Freedom from unwanted pregnancies is, moreover, itself a basic need. If met, it reduces, not desired family size, but fertility rates, by reducing the number of unwanted births. For these three reasons—saving resources on objectives with lower priority than BN, economizing on linkages, and reducing fertility rates (and, on certain assumptions, population growth)—BN economizes in the use of resources or in the time needed to satisfy basic needs.

BN will also tend to make more resources available, both domestically and (possibly) internationally. More resources will be available domestically for four reasons. First, the composition of output needed to satisfy basic needs is likely to be produced more labor-intensively. In countries with underemployed labor, this will raise not only employment, but also production. Second, an attack on malnutrition, disease, and illiteracy not only lengthens life and improves its quality (desirable in their own right) but also improves the quality of the labor force. It is, however, an open question whether the returns from this form of human investment are higher, at the margin, than those from more conventional investment in physical capital. Third, the removal of motives for large families, by an attack on "correlates of fertility decline," mentioned in the previous paragraphs, can be alternatively regarded as a factor reducing the required resources as well as increasing the available resources. Fourth, a BN approach that is based on participation will mobilize local resources and increase incentives for higher production.

More resources may be available internationally because the pledge for meeting the basic needs of the world's poor as a first charge on our aid budgets has stronger moral and political appeal than most other schemes advanced for the promotion of international assistance. There can be no certainty about this, but it is already clear that the concept has international appeal and may help to overcome the present aid fatigue by defining new forms of international cooperation and commitment.[5] Since food is an important element in BN, and since, given the distribution of votes in Western democracies, food aid is politically easier to provide than financial aid, properly channeled food aid can make an important international contribution to meeting BN.

It remains to be investigated how a BN approach is likely to affect specific resource constraints such as foreign exchange, administrative skills, etc. It might be thought that BN would reduce exports, but it would also tend to reduce import requirements. It would certainly call for more administrative skills, but if local energy can be harnessed, motivation for raising the supply of those skills would be strengthened. And, those skills might not need to be of a particularly sophisticated kind and therefore might be speedily acquired.

In brief, therefore, a BN approach, because it saves resources, because it mobilizes more resources, and because it makes these resources more productive achieves an agreed-upon priority objective sooner than a solely income-oriented approach, even if it is poverty weighted. The BN "resource gap" is narrowed or closed from both ends.

But two crucial questions remain, one of value and one of fact. The value assumption underlying the above argument is that zero weight (or at least substantially lower weight) is attached to the uses of all extra resources that do not meet basic needs. It may be objected that governments and people who do not accept this value judgment will reject the whole approach and those that do accept it, won't need it. But aid agencies might wish to adopt it, and governments and people do not have monolithic value systems. By dialogue and pressures they might be pushed in the direction of accepting the value judgment.

The crucial factual assumption is that leakages or "trickle-up" in a selective system are smaller than in a general system. If the benefits do not effectively reach the needy, the wastage of the BN approach may be as large as, or even larger than, that of the income-oriented, nonselective approach. This is an important area for operational research and experimentation.

The Politics of Basic Needs

It is sometimes argued that BN is an ideological (polemical, religious, emotive) concept that conceals a call to revolution. Such an interpretation can be justified neither historically nor analytically. (Even if it could be justified, it would still require a delivery system for the revolution.) It is evident that a wide variety of political regimes have satisfied basic needs within a relatively short time. Options for the future are even more varied than the limited experiences of the past twenty-five years.

It is true, of course, that the success of these different political regimes in meeting basic needs cannot be attributed to their having written BN on their banner. But they share certain initial conditions (in the distribution of assets, levels of education and health, etc.) and a set of policies that present important lessons to others attempting to meet basic needs. The fact that they started from a base at which some basic needs for health and education were already satisfied obviously reduced the time required for meeting basic needs, both directly and through their indirect effect on the quality and motivation of the labor force.

If some political regimes have succeeded in satisfying basic needs within a short period of time without adopting the BN approach as an explicit policy instrument, others have paid lip service to the objective without succeeding in implementing it. The reasons for this gap between profession and practice are, ultimately, political. To some extent, it might be objected, governments lack the knowledge and administrative power to meet basic needs. Rural development programs are far more difficult to administer than those for the urban elite, though the same governments are often capable of administering complex programs of import restrictions or investment licensing, where the protection of the privileged is in question. The neglect might also be explained partly by the system of incentives and the type of technologies considered to be essential to a development strategy. But neither administrative weakness nor incentives and technology can fully account for what must ultimately be attributed to absence of a political base. High marginal tax rates, paid by very few, and land reform legislation that remains unimplemented are the result not so much of administrative weakness or belief in the need for incentives, as they are the result of the fact that the rich operate the machinery to what they regard as their advantage.

If the failures of past strategies are due to vested interests and to the political obstruction of those who would lose from a basic-needs approach, it becomes essential to show how these forces can be kept in check. In many regimes the poor are weak bargainers and are not a political constituency. But measures to meet basic needs can be implemented by a reformist alliance, in a peaceful manner. Some of these measures are clearly in the narrow self-interest of the dominant groups, such as the eradication of communicable diseases or the preservation of social peace. Others are in the longer-term interest of some groups who would have to mobilize support for gradual reform. In nineteenth-century England, the rural rich campaigned against the urban rich for factory legislation, which improved the condition of the poor, while the urban rich campaigned against the rural rich for the repeal of the Corn Laws, which reduced the price of food for the poor. Urban industrialists and workers may support a land reform benefiting small farmers and landless laborers, if this promises more food.

It is possible, however, that the mobilization of the rural and urban masses required for this approach could initiate a revolutionary process which the initiators of the mobilization process might regret. The conditions in which this is liable to happen and the conditions in which a grass-roots democracy on a pluralist model might emerge have received almost no attention so far.

Nor have the macroeconomic implications of the transition from the present state to one in which basic needs are met been thoroughly investigated. Inflationary pressures, redirection of demand toward basic-needs goods in inelastic supply, increased imports, capital flight, brain drain, or strikes by disaffected groups could present obstacles in the path of implementation.

Whatever the route, a BN approach, having identified the political, administrative, and institutional obstacles to fulfilling basic needs, must specify how these constraints are to be removed.

Supply Management

It has been argued that a distinguishing feature of the BN approach is that it is not sufficient to channel purchasing power into the hands of the poor through employment creation, productivity-raising measures, improvements in access to productive factors for the self-employed, and appropriate policies for relative prices. The structure of production must be such that it responds speedily to the demand generated for basic needs. The issue here is whether additional direct interventions in the productive system are then required.

There are merits in a system that relies on raising the productivity of the poor sufficiently to channel purchasing power to them and then permits prices and market forces to allocate supplies. No objections in principle are commonly raised against using selective price policies (indirect taxes and subsidies) to steer consumer and producer choices in the direction of meeting basic needs. Experience in some countries has shown that attempts to interfere directly with supply by rationing, licensing, building permits or other direct controls have been open to abuse and have at best bred inefficiency. At worst they have strengthened monopoly power, increased inequality, and encouraged corruption. Yet, it may be necessary to combine the generation of earning opportunities with some forms of direct supply management in order to prevent the intentions of demand policy from being frustrated. The purpose of higher money incomes for the poor can be frustrated by rising prices of the goods and services on which they spend their income if additional supply is not forthcoming, so that real incomes do not improve (e.g., when improved agricultural prices lead to higher prices of industrial products bought by farmers). Or the higher money incomes of one group of poor may be met by extra supplies, but only at the expense of another group which then suffers from deprivation.

The disadvantages of rationing and other direct controls have been examined largely in the light of the efficient allocation of resources for productivity and growth, though there has been some work on the impact of such controls on employment and income distribution. There has been hardly any work, however, on the scope and limits of these instruments for the purpose of meeting basic needs. A reassessment may well lead to the modification of some of the conclusions.

Changes in relative prices are useful instruments for marginal adjustments, but they are not always equally suitable for bringing about discrete changes. And the transition from the present state to a basic-needs-oriented approach will call for large and fairly sudden changes. Total prohibition of the import and the domestic production of a non–basic-needs item is often a better way of controlling its consumption (and, indirectly, its technology and income distribution) than a tariff combined with an excise tax, if policing to prevent smuggling and bootlegging is effective. Since controls can only prevent activities, not induce them, the positive counterpart to controls may be production in the public sector.

According to one interpretation of BN, the domestic structure of production must be adapted to BN requirements. If this were to imply forgoing the benefits from foreign trade, such an interpretation would be nonsense, of course. "Supply management" must cover wholesale and retail distribution, transport and storage, and foreign trade. But a needs-oriented approach may raise previously neglected issues in interregional and international trade. Thus, if it were found that the poor in scattered rural communities cannot purchase the food grains imported from abroad (or produced in the most efficient areas domestically) because, in comparing costs, the costs of transport, distribution, and storage were not fully taken into account, it may well turn out that the food should be locally produced, even at what may appear to be somewhat higher costs.[6]

Implementation: Trickle-up

Some critics of the BN approach share the goal of meeting basic needs but object that, unless specific steps that lead to their satisfaction are spelled out, it cannot be called a strategy. This is an entirely valid invitation to think through the implications of a BN approach. No doubt there is nothing yet that could be described as a fully articulated BN strategy, even as an adjunct to other strategies. For those who agree on the objective, the conclusions ought to be (a) further work in areas of ignorance (see below) and (b) experimentation with a wide variety of approaches in the initial stages, so that experience from pilot projects will be gathered for replication.

One of the inadequacies of past approaches is that they have not done full justice to the precise impact of public services on satisfying needs. The study of how public services can reach the poor and how the poor can mobilize their own efforts to make these services effective is still in a rudimentary state. The questions to be answered are: How can we insure that public revenues, devoted to public services to meet BN, actually reach the vulnerable groups? How is access to the bureaucracy secured? How can we determine priorities in the line of applicants? What system of checks against abuse and of monitoring to insure success is required?

While the biased impact of social services for the poor has received a good deal of attention, the biased impact of many systems of taxation has received less attention. Either taxes do not exist, or nominal taxes are not collected, or, where they are collected, their ultimate incidence is shifted onto those least able to bear them. Thorough scrutiny of the system of collecting revenues and the incidence of taxation from the point of view of meeting basic needs is as important as examining the incidence of public services.

Linkages, Complementarities, and Trade-offs

The improvement of nutrition, or of water supply, or of sanitation, or of health services, each in isolation, may have a smaller impact on the mortality or morbidity of a poverty group than a concerted attack. Without adequate nutrition, resistance to disease will be lower and the cost of a health program higher. Without the elimination of gastrointestinal diseases, nutritional requirements are higher. Without safe water, control of communicable disease, and improvements in public health, nutritional programs are unlikely to have permanent benefits. There is evidence that family-planning programs are more effective if combined with nutrition and health measures. The benefits of education in raising the effective impact of all other services is obvious. And equally, improved nutrition and health services enable children to benefit more from education.

Certain linkages between different public services reduce costs; others improve the impact. In addition, there are important and sometimes neglected linkages between private income and access to public services. Parents have to earn adequate incomes before they can afford to spare their children from work and send them to school, and they need money to equip them with books and to transport them, and to provide them with properly lit rooms for their homework. The sick must be able to afford to travel to clinics.

Therefore, while a concerted attack on several fronts or a "big push" is more effective, policies have to be selective because resources are scarce. Alternatively, there may be trade-offs between, say, eradicating malaria and some other operation. In such cases a "vertical," or spearhead, approach would be more appropriate than a "horizontal" approach. This implies that the quantification of the costs and benefits of these services must be conducted in terms of selective packages. The implications for project appraisal are clear. Costs per unit of a given public service may be reduced if the service is combined with others, and the impact on health, education, nutrition, or family planning may be raised by such a combination. For some purposes, "balanced growth" may be more economical; for others an "unbalanced" attack may be best. Detailed investigation of these issues is an essential feature of the successful implementation of a BN approach.

Technologies and Administration

The cost of providing for basic needs will vary over a wide range, depending on the technology. But the technology, in turn, will depend on the degree of local initiative, commitment, and participation; the amount and quality of local factors of production and materials mobilized; and local cultural attitudes and social institutions. The managerial and administrative framework for implementing BN is crucial for its feasibility and costs. There is much talk about the need for participation and self-management. The important questions, however, relate to the precise combination of central leadership, decentralized decisionmaking, and mobilization of local resources (especially underemployed, low-cost labor) which would be most effective in specific circumstances.

There is also the question of what forms participation should take in a democracy. The fascist corporate state claimed that it drew on the participation of workers, employers, and farmers. It has been said (by Peter Wiles) that Tito got the idea of self-managed enterprises from Mussolini. Whether true or not, self-management has been practised more in socialist dictatorships than in democracies. There are forms of participation that bypass representative democratic institutions.

Past calculations have often started by counting those in need and estimating the cost of eliminating the deficiency. The counting was often wrong (in view of the poor data base) and the standards of what was supposed to be supplied were often ill chosen. The resulting bill for "needed services" was exorbitant and, in practice, the partial attempts to provide them rarely succeeded in reaching the poor. Planning for BN should set standards that are correct and allow for the wide interpersonal and intertemporal variations in human requirements; it should pay attention to what can be afforded by the use of appropriate technologies; it should pay attention to social and cultural forces, mobilize local resources, and concentrate on processes and sequences that meet the needs of the poor. The "count, cost, and carry" approach has little to contribute to this. The correct approach is still largely unexplored.

Allowing for individual variations in energy requirements reduces the estimated shortfalls. As P. V. Sukhatme has shown, the incidence of undernutrition for India comes to 25 percent for urban areas and 15 percent for rural areas (compare the estimates of 50 percent and 40 percent, respectively, made by Dandekar and Rath based on a poverty line corresponding to average requirements).[7]

Time-Discount Rates and Poverty Weighting

A distinct feature of the BN approach is its structure of time-discount rates. The structure will register how many extra dollars we are prepared to sacrifice in 1 year's, 5 years', or 20 years' time for an extra 100 dollars today. Implicit in the BN approach is a high rate of time discount for the near future, reflecting the urgency of meeting basic needs soon, subject to maintaining achieved satisfactions of basic needs indefinitely.

The first strategy ("consumption transfers") simulated in Ahluwalia and Chenery's "Model of Redistribution and Growth"[8] captures the essence of a strategy that goes for short-run payoffs. On the assumptions of this model, which exaggerates some of the shortcomings of this approach, as the authors admit, the consumption levels of the poor are substantially above the basic solution for the first 25 years, but after that the growth of the income of the poor is reduced not only below that of the investment transfer solution, but also the basic solution. To the extent, however, that meeting the basic needs of children, e.g., by school feeding programs, is an investment in the future labor force, and that meeting basic needs reduces the rate of population growth, the approach yields returns after 15 to 30 years. The operational implication of this is that measures to raise the consumption of the poor now and in the future, as long as they are conducted on a sustainable basis, compensate for the reduction in capital formation below what it would otherwise have been by the bonus we derive from investing in future generations and reducing population growth.

Another distinct feature is the weighting of meeting the basic needs of those at different distances below the basic-needs standard. Previous approaches either simply count the heads of those below a defined poverty line, without distinguishing degrees of deprivation among them, or attach differential weights to income growth of different deciles. A. K. Sen has suggested a weighted measure of the income shortfalls below the basic needs line.[9] He takes the rank value of the poor in the income ranking as the weights to be put on the income shortfalls of the different persons in the category of the poor. If there are m people with incomes below the basic needs line, the income shortfalls of the richest among the poor gets a weight of 1, the second richest a weight of 2, and so on, ending up with a weight of m on the shortfall of the poorest poor. This measure has the virtue of being sensitive to the exact pattern of the income shortfalls of the poor from the basic-needs line.

But we have argued that income is an inadequate and only partial guide to basic needs. We need to supplement the above approach by taking explicit account of which goods and services are going to whom. Again, Sen has suggested that "commodity j going to person i may be thought to be a good ij in itself, not the same as the same commodity going to another person k, which is now taken to be a different good, ik. . . . The approach can, of course, be married also to that of dealing with characteristics such as calories as opposed to specific commodities such as rice or bajra."[10] In this manner, weights would be attached not to income but to specified goods and services or even to the impact on specified basic needs.

A pure BN approach would give zero weight to meeting the needs of those above the basic-needs line, until the basic needs of all are met. But if the BN approach is regarded as an adjunct to other strategies, the relative weight to be attached to income growth of those above the basic-needs line remains to be determined by the policymakers. To illustrate: a pure BN approach would sacrifice any amount of capital accumulation if thereby the BN of all could be satisfied on a sustainable basis, within a short period. A mixed strategy might prefer to leave the BN of 5 percent unsatisfied, if thereby sustained growth of income above basic needs could be attained for the remaining 95 percent.

II. Basic Needs and Growth: A Trade-Off?

Critics of the BN approach to development often complain that such an approach would sacrifice savings, productive investment, and incentives to work, for the sake of current consumption and welfare; that poor countries can ill afford such a sacrifice; and that, in any case, the advocates of BN should bring out the choice clearly, so that the costs in terms of forgone growth can be seen.

BN and growth are not strictly comparable objectives. Growth emphasizes annual increments of production and income, and concern for the future. A BN approach must also contain a time dimension. It proposes a set of policies that increasingly meet a dynamic range of the basic needs of a growing population.

If BN and growth are to be compared at all, the questions should be: Does meeting basic needs imply sacrificing certain components of current output or certain components of current incomes? Such a sacrifice then may reduce aggregate growth of income per head by raising the capital/output ratio, and/or by lowering the savings ratio, and/or by raising population growth. Four types of trade-offs can be envisaged:

(1) There may be a trade-off between benefits to higher-income groups in favor of benefits to lower-income groups.

(2) There may be a trade-off between non–basic-needs goods and services consumed by *all* income groups, including the poor, in favor of basic-needs goods and services consumed by the poor.

(3) There may be a trade-off between activities that create incentives for larger savings and efforts to work (incentive goods, private savings, budget surplus) in favor of current consumption.

(4) There may be a trade-off between goods and services which make a larger contribution to future production in favor of those that make a smaller contribution or no contribution.

Trade-offs (3) and (4) would mean sacrificing future production in favor of current consumption. All policies have certain distributional dimensions in both space and time: they imply decisions about how goods and services are distributed between income groups, between regions, between occupations, and, of course, over time. The concern of those who suspect that BN involves a trade-off with growth is that the children and grandchildren of those whose basic needs are met now would have to accept lower levels of living than if the present generation were asked to tighten its belt more and postpone meeting basic needs for higher prosperity later.

BN draws attention to a principal objective of development, which is to eradicate poverty. This logical precedence of an end over the means of achieving this end in no way implies that the means can be neglected. On the contrary, it focuses attention on the means required to achieve the end. Although there is a welfare component in BN, to meet BN on a sustainable basis in poor countries calls for considerable investment and growth of production in addition to structural reforms; but this growth would be differently composed and distributed (and may be differently measured) than non–BN-oriented growth. Growth is also required to meet the rising standards of BN as income rise and new needs supplement those already satisfied, and to achieve objectives other than BN, such as rising prosperity for the less poor, non–basic-needs satisfaction for all, provision for the prosperity of future generations, provision for national defense, etc.

It is important to note that BN itself has three production- and productivity-raising consequences, which have not yet been precisely quantified. First, a well-nourished, healthy, vigorous, educated, skilled labor force is a more efficient and better-motivated labor force than one whose basic needs have not been met.[11] Second, BN contains thrusts which are important correlates of fertility decline, such as women's education, reduced infant mortality (which leads rapidly to reduced desired family size), and health. Even the purest welfare component of the approach, social security for the aged, sick, and disabled, may have an important influence on reducing desired family size by reducing the incentive to have children as a source of support. Third, BN for the mass of the people can be met only by a large-scale mobilization of under-utilized local labor and materials. Economy in the use of existing resources and augmentation of these resources through massive investment in human capital, fertility decline, and mobilization of local under-utilized resources are important resource-saving and resource-augmenting consequences of BN. If a BN approach were to mobilize additional international resources, this would be a further source of augmentation.

Ignoring for the moment problems of measurement, we can illustrate the options by four paths (Figure 1). On the diagram we trace the log of consumption per head of the poor on the vertical axis and time on the horizontal axis (so that a straight line shows growth at a constant proportionate rate). Path 1 starts with lower levels of consumption but, as a result of better incentives and productive investment, it overtakes path 2 at some time T_1 and then for ever after, the consumption of the poor is higher. Path 2 starts with higher consumption by the poor but, by neglecting incentives, private and public savings, and productive investment, it falls behind path 1 after a certain date, T_1 . This is how the option is often presented and how it has also been implemented in a few countries.

It should be clear that sound policies should rule out path 3, which lies consistently below both path 1 and path 2. This could be the result of inefficient ways of meeting the needs of the poor, in which both current consumption and future consumption are lower than on the alternative paths. (There clearly are also inefficient paths in the pursuit of investment and growth.)

The rationale behind BN, however, is path 4. High priority is given to some components of current consumption of the poor which may then, for a while, fall below the consumption level that could have been attained by a more growth-oriented strategy. But when the present generation of children is entering the labor force and human capital begins to yield returns at time T_2 , the growth path is steeper than it would have been under

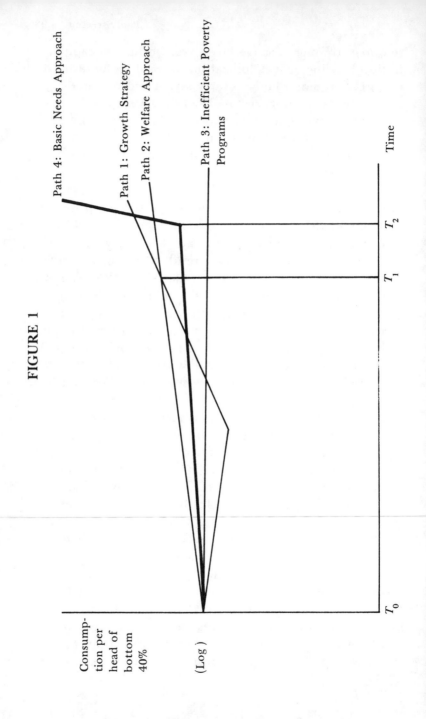

FIGURE 1

1, and overtakes first the welfare path 2 and later the
growth path 1.

Forced industrialization under Stalin and the Industrial
Revolution in England followed path 1. Taiwan, Korea,
and perhaps, Japan followed path 4, in earlier years laying
the runway for future "take-off into self-sustained growth"
by meeting certain basic needs through land reform and
massive investment in human capital, especially education.
Critics charge that Sri Lanka and Tanzania may be following path 2 and Burma path 3, though these experiences
have not yet been fully analyzed.

In comparing growth paths, it is important that growth
and its components are correctly measured. Basic needs are
measured, in the first place, in terms of physiological needs
and physical inputs—so many primary school teachers, so
many paramedical workers, so many calories—and financial
costs are calculated from these. Growth, on the other
hand, is an aggregate in which the existing, often very
unequal, income distribution determines purchasing power
and with it the price weights. A 10 percent increase in
the income of a man who earns $10,000 is weighted a
hundred times as much as a 10 percent increase in the
income of a man with $100. In *Redistribution with
Growth,* Chenery et al. have suggested modifications to
the conventional growth measure, which weights initial
shares of each income group by their share in the national income, so that the weight of the poorest is the
smallest and that of the richest the largest. One possibility is to weight each group equally, according to the
number of people (or households, allowing for size and
age distribution) in it, so that a 1 percent growth of the
poorest 25 percent has the same weight as 1 percent
growth of the richest 25 percent. An even more radical
system of weighting would attribute zero weights to the
growth of income of all income groups above the poorest
25 or 40 percent and a weight of unity to those below

the poverty line. Whatever method is chosen, any discussion of the trade-off between BN and growth ought to specify what weights it attaches to income growth of different income groups. This would bring out clearly the value judgments underlying the strategy.

The relative importance of different items in the consumption basket is normally determined by their relative prices. We register growth when the consumption of whiskey has risen, even though the consumption of milk has declined. This is not because we regard whiskey consumed by the rich as more important than milk consumed by the poor, but because the higher incomes of the rich determine the relatively high price of whiskey, while the lack of purchasing power of the poor is reflected in the low price of milk. In societies with unequal income distribution, the standard measure for GNP growth, therefore, gives excessive weight to the growth of non-basic-needs goods and deficient weight to basic-needs goods.

There is, however, a complication that does not arise from problems of measurement. It may be thought necessary to neglect the welfare of the poor people in the short run and possibly even in the medium run in order to permit the nonpoor to make money, for this is what benefits the poor in the long run. In fact, this is a choice that some countries may have to face when the institutions meant to reach the poor directly are still weak and disorganized: for instance, a choice may have to be made between establishing large-scale industries now or waiting indefinitely for small-scale enterprise to emerge.

Certain forms of the "trickle-down" approach have been discredited, but there are a number of mechanisms by which the wealth of the nonpoor could benefit the poor: expanded demand for their labor, higher wages or lower prices resulting from productivity growth, upgrading of skills, tax revenues collected from the rich and spent on social services or transfers, etc. There is now firm evidence that, as far as agriculture for food production is concerned, inequality of land holdings is not a necessary condition of raising yields per acre or even (above a critical minimum size) yields per unit of all inputs, but the same may not be true of the industrial sector. Where encouraging the better-off to improve their position now is regarded as a necessary condition for improving the lot of the poor later, a genuine conflict between BN and growth arises. In such cases, the countries concerned will have to make pragmatic choices, but they must also insure that the increased productivity of the nonpoor is to some extent redirected to benefit the poor and that the ultimate goal of channeling resources directly to increase the productivity of the poor is not wholly forgotten in the process.

We conclude that one difference between growth strategies and basic-needs strategies consists in the content of growth and its beneficiaries. Conventionally measured economic growth uses weights that show no concern for what is produced and consumed, or for whose benefits. A dollar's worth of purchasing power is counted the same, whether it is spent on whiskey or milk or whether it is spent by the affluent or by deprived children. BN puts the needs of the poor into the center. If this is reflected in a proper measure, what at first appears as a trade-off may turn out not to be one.

At the same time, growth is a necessary component of a BN approach because:

(1) Permitting the better-off to accumulate may be a necessary condition for meeting basic needs.

(2) Not all BN can be satisfied at once, even by the most radical redistribution of income and restructuring of production, so that growth is needed to meet them.

(3) Needs represent a hierarchy in which the satisfaction of dominant ones brings new ones to the fore.

(4) BN is a minimum program, to which other objectives will normally be added.

(5) With increasing population, more resources are needed in order to maintain present standards.

But, when particular resources needed for the particular target groups have been specified, and a time profile for meeting the basic needs of a growing population on a sustainable basis has been defined, growth will turn out to be the *result* of a basic needs policy, not its *objective*. Growth is not normally something that has to be sacrificed or traded off in order to meet present needs. On the contrary, in the light of the above considerations, a basic-needs approach may well call for *higher* growth rates than a so-called growth strategy. But the composition and the beneficiaries (and the measure) of such growth will be different from those of a conventional high-growth strategy.

III. Basic Needs and Human Rights

On the relationship between basic human rights and basic needs, Abraham Maslow had the following to say: "It is legitimate and fruitful to regard instinctoid basic needs and the metaneeds as rights as well as needs. This follows immediately upon granting that human beings have a right to be human in the sense that cats have a right to be cats. In order to be fully human, these need and metaneed gratifications are necessary, and may therefore be considered to be natural rights."[12] This is not a very fortunate way of making the point. If being human is a fact, the question of rights does not arise. If, on the other hand, unlike cats, to be human is to aspire to an ideal (it makes sense to say "Be a man!" but it does not make sense to say "Be a cat!") the provision of the conditions for fulfilling this aspiration may be regarded as a right.

Material needs, narrowly interpreted, can be met in ways which conflict with rights, as when a society is

organized as a prison or a zoo. And rights may conflict
with needs, as when freedom of expression and free elec-
tions prevent a radical land reform or tax reform or any
other redistribution to the poor. In a democracy in which
each votes according to his self-interest and there are no
rich-poor alliances, the poor will never have enough votes
to get redistribution to them enacted. As Nozick has
shown, the top 49 percent can always persuade the middle,
swing vote of 2 percent by adequate compensation not to
join the bottom 49 percent, so that redistribution toward
the middle, but not toward the poor, is the result. Experience from democratic countries confirms the a priori
reasoning.

There is also an ambiguity between interpreting basic
needs as material preconditions and fundamental human
requirements for fulfillment. "I give you the toast of the
Royal Economic Society, of economics and economists,
who are the trustees not of civilization but of the possibility of civilization." So Keynes toasted the Royal Economic Society at the dinner in 1945. Substitute basic
needs for civilization, and we must ask: Can or should
the state actually satisfy basic needs, or should it provide
only the possibility of their satisfaction? This question is,
of course, closely related to the previous one about needs
and rights, for some forms of satisfaction are possible only
at the expense of rights, and some rights are inconsistent
with actual need fulfillment.

IV. Basic Needs and the
New International Economic Order

Members of the Group of 77 are apprehensive lest a
basic-needs approach adopted by donors imply sacrificing
features of the New International Economic Order (NIEO).
Sceptics among the developed countries regard both the

NIEO and BN as highly charged emotional words without clear policy implications.

It is true that on superficial inspection there appears to be a conflict. The NIEO aims at revising the rules of international economic relations so as to provide more equal opportunities to all *governments*, whereas basic needs is concerned with the needs of *individuals* and households. The NIEO deals with issues such as commodity-price stabilization and support, indexation, the common fund, the integrated commodity program, debt relief, the SDR link, trade liberalization, trade preferences, technology transfer, etc., whereas BN deals with food, water, health, education, and shelter. The NIEO aims at unconditional, automatic or semiautomatic, concealed transfers of resources (or at correcting past reverse transfers), whereas basic needs implies a highly targeted approach, aiming directly at the alleviation of deprivation of particular groups. The NIEO would eliminate conditions imposed on resource transfers; BN would wish to make transfers conditional upon their reaching the poor. The schemes proposed in the NIEO are likely to benefit the middle-income countries and some very small (already relatively overaided) countries in whose economy foreign trade plays an important part, rather than the large, poor countries of Asia. Moreover, within the beneficiary countries, the proposed NIEO schemes are likely to benefit the higher-income groups, such as exporting industrialists and large farmers, rather than the urban and rural poor.

But the conflict can be avoided. The differences between the two approaches point to the need to advance on both fronts simultaneously. The NIEO is concerned with formulating a framework of institutions, processes, and rules that would correct what developing countries regard as the present bias of the system against them. This bias is thought to be evident in the structure of certain markets, where a few large and powerful buyers confront many weak, competing sellers; in discrimination in access to capital markets and access to knowledge; in the present patent law and patent conventions; in the thrust of research and development and the nature of modern technology; in the power of the transnational corporations; in international monetary arrangements, etc. A correction in the direction of a more balanced distribution of power and access to power would enable developing countries to become less dependent and more self-reliant. But the NIEO by itself would be no guarantee that the governments of the developing countries would use their new power to meet the needs of their poor. The BN approach, by focusing on deprived individuals, households, and communities, highlights the importance of the needs of individual human beings.

A BN program that does not build on the self-reliance and self-help of governments and countries is in danger of degenerating into a global charity program. A NIEO that is not committed to meeting basic needs is liable to transfer resources from the poor in rich countries to the rich in poor countries.

It is easy to envisage situations in which the benefits of international BN assistance are more than wiped out by the damage done by protectionist trade measures, by an unequal distribution of the gains from trade and foreign investment, by transfer pricing practices of multinationals, by the unemployment generated by inappropriate technology, or by restrictive monetary policies. The global commitment to BN makes sense only in an international order in which the impact of all other international policies—trade, foreign investment, technology transfer, movement of professionals, money—is not detrimental to meeting basic needs.

The situation is similar to the rise of trade unions in nineteenth-century England. Concern with the fate of the poor remained relatively ineffective until the poor were permitted by law to organize themselves, bargain collectively, strike, and have their funds protected. On the other hand, there has always been the danger that trade unions would turn into another powerful estate, less concerned with the fate of the poor than with protecting the privileges of a labor aristocracy.

The NIEO is a framework of rules and institutions, regulating the relations between sovereign nations, and BN is one important objective which this framework should serve. The way to make the institutions serve the objective is to strike a bargain: donors will accept features of the NIEO if, and only if, developing countries commit themselves to a BN approach.

A more specific question is how an international BN approach is to be implemented in a manner consistent with the spirit of the NIEO. The governments of developing countries are anxious to preserve their full sovereignty and autonomy and do not wish to have their priorities laid down for them by donors. They dislike strings attached to aid and close scrutiny of its use. Donors, on the other hand, wish to make sure that their contributions reach the people for whom they are intended. The solution is to be found in the strengthening of existing institutions and the evolution of new institutions, acceptable to both donors and recipients, that insure that international aid reaches the vulnerable groups. Such buffer institutions and buffer processes would combine full national sovereignty with BN priority. They would be representative, independent, and genuinely devoted to the goals of international cooperation.

It is clear that only multilateral institutions can meet these conditions. But reform may be required on several issues. The distribution of votes must be such that the developing countries feel that they are fairly represented. The selection, recruitment, and training of members of the international secretariat must be of a kind which transcends narrow national loyalties but is sensitive to the social and cultural issues in developing countries. Both narrow technocracy and an excessive politicization of issues must be avoided. It may be thought that this amounts to a prescription for perfection; but international institutions and their secretariats have, in some instances, approximated these ideal canons. Unless they do, there is little hope of implementing BN in the framework of the NIEO.

V. The Case for Additional
Official Development Assistance (ODA)
to Finance Basic Needs

Provisional and very rough estimates indicate that a basic-needs program aiming at providing minimum acceptable diets, safe water, sewerage facilities, public health measures, basic education, and the upgrading of existing shelter would call for an annual investment of $20 billion over a twenty-year period (1980-2000) at 1976 prices. If recurrent expenditures are added, the annual total costs would amount to $45-60 billion. If programs are implemented only in the poorest countries, annual investment and recurrent costs are estimated to be $30-40 billion. This would be 12-16 percent of these countries' projected GNP and 80-100 percent of their projected gross investment. Assuming the OECD countries concentrate their efforts on the poorest countries and contribute about 50 percent of the additional costs of these programs, this would call for $15-20 billion ODA flows per year over twenty years.

At present, ODA flows from OECD countries amount to about $14 billion a year. Of this, the poorest countries receive only about $6 billion. The question arises why the whole of this flow or some part of it should not be devoted to BN and why the flow to middle-income countries should not be devoted to the poor countries.

Only a part of this assistance is at present devoted to meeting BN, and the resource calculations are based on *additional* requirements. Nevertheless, it might be asked why the whole of the assistance should not be switched to what is agreed to be a priority objective, so that additional requirements could be greatly reduced. If, moreover, some ODA now going to middle-income countries could be redirected to the poorest countries, requirements could be further reduced.

Such redirection would, however, be neither desirable nor possible. Middle-income countries have a higher absorptive capacity and tend to show higher returns on resource transfers. They, too, have serious problems of poverty. Moreover, a reallocation of ODA flows is politically much easier if it is done out of incremental flows than if existing flows to some countries have to be cut. The legacy of past commitments and the expectations that they have generated cannot be discarded in a few years.

There are three reasons why additional resources of about $20 billion per year (on average over the period 1980–2000) are needed in order to make a convincing international contribution to BN programs in the poorest countries. First, twenty years is a very short time for a serious antipoverty program. It calls for extra efforts on the part of both developed and developing countries. The domestic effort—economic, administrative, and political—required from the developing countries is formidable. At the same time, while the figures for ODA seem large, total ODA flows that would rise year by year by $2 billion between 1980 and 2000 (averaging $20 billion per year for the whole 20 years) would still be only 0.43 percent of the GNP of the OECD countries in 2000, substantially below the target of 0.7 percent. The acceleration (from the present 0.34 percent) is certainly within the power of the developed countries and, if the task is to be taken seriously by both sides, an increase of the percentage of GNP by 26 percent over 20 years appears to be a reasonable basis for mutual reassurance.

The second reason for additionality is that the transition from present policies to a basic-needs approach creates formidable problems of transition. Investment projects that have been started cannot suddenly be terminated. An attempt to switch to basic-needs programs while the structure of demand and production has not yet been adapted to them is bound to create inflationary and balance-of-payments pressures. There might be capital flight and added brain drain as social groups that anticipate being hurt attempt to safeguard their interests. There might be strikes from disaffected workers in the organized industrial sector. Unless a government has some resources to overcome these transitional difficulties, the attempt to embark on a BN program might be nipped in the bud.

The third reason for additionality is tactical and political. It is well known that the developing countries are suspicious of the BN approach. One reason for their suspicion is that they believe that pious words conceal a desire to opt out of development assistance. There is no doubt that some people in the developed world see BN as a cheap option. If the international commitment to meet basic needs within a short period is to be taken seriously by the developing countries, the contribution by the developed country must be additional and substantial. The essence of the Global Compact, announced by Mr. McNamara in Manila in 1976, is that both developed and developing countries should reach a basic understanding to meet human needs of the absolute poor within a reasonable period of time. Such a compact would be a sham if it did not involve substantial additional capital transfers.

VI. The Role of Global Models

Attempts have been made not only to estimate resource requirements for meeting basic needs but also to design global models. Perhaps the best known one is *Catastrophe or New Society*, the report of a multidisciplinary group based on Bariloche, Argentina, under the direction of Amilcar Herrera. The Bariloche model contains certain novel and attractive features relevant to a BN approach.

First, it is explicitly normative and rests on the premise that the satisfaction of basic human needs is the main objective of development. These needs are defined as nutrition, housing, education, and health. They are defined not in consumerist terms but as prerequisites for the ability of every individual to take a full and active part in his or her social and cultural environment.

Second, the maximand in the model is life expectancy, a healthy counterweight to GNP per head and the first approximation to a system of social and demographic accounts which, in principle, can be enriched in a sensible way by adding periods of time within the average life expectancy spent in primary and secondary school, at university, in employment, in retirement, in hospital, on vacation, in prison, on an analyst's couch, in a single, married, divorced, or widowed state, etc. (clearly, the system would fail to capture some of the choices and trade-offs that GNP per head does, but it would serve as a useful complement).

Third, population is endogenously determined by the degree of satisfaction of basic needs. And, fourth, like a number of other global studies, it is a protest against the implicit recommendation of *Limits to Growth* that developing countries must stop developing in order to prevent pollution, raw material exhaustion, and the End of the World.

Apart from the explicitly normative nature of the model, its most interesting feature is its attempt to correct excessive emphasis on maximizing GNP or growth (nonsense objectives) by maximizing life expectancy. Since life expectancy has, unlike income distribution, an upper limit shared by all, just over 70 years, a rise in the average does say something significant about meeting certain basic needs of the whole population, though we can clearly live longer and yet more miserable lives. Dispersions remain relevant but extreme skewness does not occur.

One trouble with the Bariloche model is that the production function by which life expectancy is maximized is somewhat odd. The terms of the equations, unlike land, labor, and capital in, say, a Cobb-Douglas production function, cannot meaningfully be substituted for each other at the margin. Thus, in the model, by increasing the urbanization rate we reduce the birth rate and raise life expectancy. Presumably therefore, there is, according to the model, some rate of substitution at which we can reduce protein and calories per person and substitute increased urbanization and reach the same life expectancy; or reduce the population in the primary sector while reducing education. Such a production function for maximizing life expectancy does not make sense. The authors say, rightly, "care must be taken not to confuse functional relationships with causal relationships. This is an empirical model that shows that there is a high correlation between demographic variables and certain socioeconomic variables, but in no way does it attempt to define the mechanisms that cause these links."[13] But in the light of this caveat, it is not clear how optimization can be achieved.

The conclusions of the Bariloche team are optimistic. The proposed world society is one in which basic human needs are satisfied. It is egalitarian, both at the national and international levels, so that growth rates in developed countries are reduced to 1–2 percent once GNP per head has reached $4,500 (in 1960 dollars), although this would reduce net transfers to developing countries (not an important contribution) and the terms of trade of the developing countries, via reduced demand for imports. Satisfying the needs of humanity along egalitarian and environmentally sound lines will then be possible in the 1990s in Latin America with a GNP per head of $809 (at 1960 prices), in 2008 in Africa with a GNP per head of $559, and in Asia in 2020, with a GNP per head of $506. There are, however, food limits in Asia which can be overcome by raising yields per acre, resorting to nonconventional food, and importing food.

It is the political assumption of the study that income is radically redistributed, which leads to the relatively low required-growth rates, low investment ratios, and speedy satisfaction of basic needs. Population growth is treated endogenously as a function of the level of living, more specifically as a function of meeting basic needs, and not as an exogenous variable. Technical progress is also incorporated. The utopian character of the political assumptions, far from detracting from the value of the exercise, is its principal attraction. The combination of detailed, scholarly scrutiny with utopian vision is all too rare and yet quite essential for progress. We need, as the sociologist Peter Berger has pleaded, more informed fantasy or pedantic utopianism, partly because political constraints can change quite suddenly and we should be technically prepared, and partly because these changes can occur only if the kind of work that the Bariloche team has done is being carried out.

The virtues and drawbacks of the formulation of global models are by now well known. They can provide a framework for organizing a large amount of data and tracing their relationships speedily. But, according to the principle of GIGO, conclusions contain no more than what has been fed into the assumptions. There is a temptation to quantify the quantifiable, to forget about the unquantified, and to proceed to suboptimize, i.e., to do perfectly something that should not be done at all. There is a lack of incentive to simplify; so that, with the aid of a computer, as Kenneth Boulding has suggested, more and more Ptolemaic epicycles would have been constructed instead of a Copernican revolution being initiated. The rigor of the specified relationships carries over into a false sense of security in relying on the conclusions. The validity of the steps in the calculations may be mistaken for the discovery of truth, and strategies may be derived from mathematical procedures.

Nevertheless, global models have their uses. While the human brain is quite good at assessing quite a large set of variables interacting in past and present situations, it is less good at predicting the effects of future changes in variables linked to one another in a complex system. The use of models lies not in prediction, or even in prophesying (which is conditional predicting, where it may be part of the intention to change the conditions and hence the predictions), but in scenario construction, which is intentionally abstracted, hypothetical implication-drawing.

The power of models in guiding choices for some of the major areas of uncertainty is limited. None of the models can help us much with decisions about genetic engineering, nuclear power, or climatic change. But the models that were formulated in protest to *Limits to Growth*, less dramatic, less apocalyptic, and sounder, are primarily justified by presenting the possibility of options. The main purpose of a good model is to show up the limitations of another model and thereby to contribute to mental flexibility. At their best, models are conceptual muscle therapy and cure us of cramps.

VII. Health Services: An Illustration of Basic Needs

The kind of evidence one would hope to gather from country, program, and sector studies can be illustrated by a comparison of the organization of health services. The

"barefoot doctors" in China are the best known example
of an "appropriate medical technology." A village appoints
one from among its members to go off for a period to be
trained and then to return and serve the community at a
rate of pay that is calculated in points, as is the rate of
pay for every other member of the team. It is important
that the health worker is not an outside bureaucrat sent
in by the government, but a full member of the commune.
There is equal access to the health services, at least within
the village, though better-off communes appear to be able
to acquire better social services.

The collective farm is not the only organization capable
of doing this. Villages with individual farming in other
parts of the world have pooled resources and provided
members of the village the means to acquire special training, but the collective farm has advantages in this form of
pooling. Clearly, there must be a corresponding decision at
the center to provide the required training for the commune's candidate. In China, the central government had
to make a conscious effort to reallocate a significant portion of its resources away from urban services toward activities that benefited rural areas.

This provision of rural health services was not delivered
as a separable and isolated benefit. The impact and cost of
these services is in many ways dependent on the provision
of basic levels of food and income. Rural health services,
for example, provide birth control information and contraceptives. The old and the sick, who were not helped much by
land reform, could draw on the welfare funds of the commune. The availability of old-age sickness benefits that do
not depend on having several surviving sons provides villagers with the incentive to use these contraceptives. The
provision of improved health services interacts with other
rural efforts, such as the mobilization of labor for rural
construction.

In India, the proposal in the draft Fifth Five-Year Plan

is to select from each village through the existing institutions of *panchayats* and *gaonsabhas* one literate individual for health training at the Primary Health Centers. Past experience, however, shows that training has been very poor, based on concepts borrowed from the West, unrelated to local practice and needs, and with high costs and poor results. The training institutions were ill equipped and under-utilized. There are problems of pay scales and of frequent transfer of personnel after training. Trained health workers (*"dais"*) apparently work for a transfer from the day they are posted to a village. *Dai* training suffered from the fact that the trainers (Lady Health Visitors and Auxiliary Nurse Midwives) competed rather than cooperated with the *dais*. The *dais*, moreover, having accepted kits and money from the government, were treated by the villagers as outside agents of the government. Neither the Center nor the states provided adequate finances to support the scheme.

Social stratification in rural areas has created its own problems. Inadequate and deficient though the medical services were, they have tended to be monopolized by the rural rich. Planners, working with the myth of a "village community," have concluded that lack of medical care for the poor is due to their indolence, inertia, and servility. Basic decisions about leadership in health administration, resource distribution (between urban, curative services and rural, preventive services, and the breaking of bottlenecks) show strong urban bias.

Some states in India are exceptions to the above characterization. Kerala has attained the lowest mortality rates and the highest life expectancy among the states in India, at a level of income per head below the average. The higher levels of nutrition are probably connected with land reforms instituted in the nineteenth century. Improved caloric intake was largely the result of higher production of tapioca. But other states show both higher caloric intake and higher per capita incomes and yet show higher mortality rates. This suggests that, in addition to other aspects of a better diet (e.g., more vegetables, fruits, fish, and eggs), other factors than nutrition may have contributed to the remarkably good health record in Kerala. The main factor is the expansion and spread of appropriate health facilities. Figures for population served by hospitals and dispensaries show a better coverage for West Bengal than for Kerala. But the proportion of persons who received treatment in hospitals and dispensaries in the two states show a utilization ratio for Kerala three-and-a-half times that of West Bengal. Much of the trouble of the health services in the rest of India is gross underutilization of existing facilities. Kerala has the highest utilization ratio. It thus achieves better results with a lower expenditure per person.

The factors responsible for the high utilization ratio have not been studied, but an important reason may be the spatial allocation of such facilities. Even if medical care is free, a person incurs direct and indirect costs in traveling to a hospital or dispensary. For those working on daily wages, a visit may mean sacrificing a day's pay. Only when the illness becomes serious enough to risk loss of employment will the journey become worthwhile. The objective of a good health care system should be to enlarge the catchment area so that the utilization ratio rises and discrimination by income and by location is reduced.

There is evidence that the high utilization ratio in Kerala is due to a location matrix that has provided the widest catchment area for its health system. In different regions of the state there is a clear correlation between number of beds per 100,000 of population and area to be covered on the one hand, and death and infant mortality rates on the other. Accessibility to medical care (by income and residence) is one of the important variables determining the level of health in a region.

Like land reforms, the policy goes back to the nineteenth

century. The Maharajah announced the following state
policy in 1865: "One of the main objects of my ambition
is to see that good medical aid is placed within the reach
of all classes of my subjects. It is a blessing which is not
at present in the power of individuals generally to secure
how much soever they may desire it. It is hence the obvious duty of the state to render its assistance in this
direction."[14]

Again, it is clear that success was due to a multipronged
attack. Side by side with medical institutions, the government of Travancore paid attention to preventive measures:
improvement of public health and sanitation, eradication
of contagious diseases, public health education, school
health inspection, etc. More than anything else, the spread
of education made the people accept the health program
of the government.

Kerala has also registered a sharp decline in birth rates.
It is not clear how far this is the result of the extension
of family-planning facilities, health services, reduced mortality rates, a rise in the age of marriage, education (especially women's education), provision for old age, or a
combination of these correlates of fertility decline (birth
rates, 1972: India, 38.4; Kerala, 31.5, per 1,000 population). It is also interesting to note that the rural-urban
difference in birth rates in Kerala (where such differences
are generally far less pronounced) was negligible in contrast to other states. The decline in the birth rate in
Kerala began in early 60s (1951–60: 38.9 per 1,000),
before the full-scale launching of the family planning
program, and may have had more to do with health and
education than with family planning facilities.

It would be quite wrong to conclude that the success
of Kerala is due primarily to measures by the communist
elements in its state governments. The origins go back to
a fairly radical land reform in the nineteenth century in
the southern part of Kerala by a local monarchy interested

in weakening the hold of feudal elements. Moreover, Kerala succeeded in meeting basic needs as a state in a nation that was less successful with central measures. Indian states with substantially better economic performance have been less successful in meeting basic needs. It is from comparisons like these that one would hope to learn useful lessons.

VIII. Transnational Corporations and Basic Needs

The role of the transnational corporation (TNC) in development is already large and is of growing importance, and policies have to be evolved that enable governments to harness its potential for the benefit of the development effort. A fundamental objective of development is to meet the basic needs of the billion or so absolute poor people in the world. Some governments are prepared to commit themselves seriously to giving high priority to this objective and wish to explore the role of TNCs in such an approach.

One of the attractions of the BN concept is that it provides a powerful organizing and integrating framework for a whole range of otherwise disparate and apparently intractable issues. One of these is the role of the TNC. When we ask ourselves what contribution TNCs can make to meeting the basic human needs of the absolute poor, the issues that are raised become, at least in principle, amenable to answers.

The BN approach consists of three components: adequate personal incomes, basic public services, and participation. The contribution of the TNC clearly lies primarily in the area of the basic–needs goods and services on which the personal incomes of the poor are spent, both producer and consumer goods, both final and intermediate products. It also covers the area in which the incomes of the poor may be earned, such as foreign trade, both in manufacturing and agriculture.

Appropriate Products

There has been a good deal of discussion of appropriate technology, and the charge has been raised that TNCs introduce excessively capital-intensive and, therefore, inappropriate technologies into the developing countries. I shall return to this issue, but the first point to make is that the oversophistication and overspecification lies more often in the *product* than in the *technology*. While the case for a "balanced diet" makes it impossible to substitute between very broadly defined product groups such as food, clothing, household goods, transport, shelter, etc., the specifications of particular products within these broadly defined groups provide scope for choice. Food can be branded and advertised, packaged, highly processed and standardized to headquarter specifications or it can be natural or semiprocessed, variable in quality, locally grown, unpackaged. Transport can be by private car, bus, motor bicycle, moped, or by bicycle. Shirts can be made with synthetic fibre and drip-dry, or with natural, locally grown fiber, washable and ironable. Agricultural machinery may be tractors or simple power tillers.

It is in the nature of the TNC that it possesses a monopolistic or oligopolistic advantage over its potential local rivals, for otherwise international investment would not occur. This oligopolistic advantage may take various forms, but one common form in consumer goods is the creation of "goodwill" through advertising and sophisticated marketing techniques, as in branded foods. Another form is the incorporation of research and development (R & D) expenditure, as in pharmaceuticals. A third form is large-scale production with the restriction on rival entry that this entails. These monopolistic advantages enable the firm to reap quasi-rents or monopoly profits until the advantage is eroded by competition, when the firm has to renew its attempt to reestablish the advantage. The sophistication of the products and the complexity of the technology determined by the products are therefore not only a response to the high incomes and high savings in the mass markets of the developed countries, but they are of the very essence of the TNC. Very simple products cannot normally be protected through patents, trademarks, trade secrets, or other forms of exclusion, and are readily imitated. Even where they can be so protected, the appropriation of profits does not last long. Unless they are much cheaper to produce on a mass scale (as is the case with buses or mopeds), the TNC has no special advantage in producing them. Why multinationals produce and sell simple basic-needs products like bicycles, sewing machines, margarine, and soap and washing powder should be investigated. Could not small-scale domestic firms, if given access to capital, other inputs, and markets, compete successfully? The presumption is that the TNC has no special advantage in supplying simple basic-needs goods and services and that transformation in the direction of reduced dualism is likely to reduce the scope for its operations.

The provision of an adequate diet and health is an essential part of the basic-needs approach. On present evidence, the branded, advertised, and marketed food products and soft drinks of the TNCs do not appear to be capable of making a substantial contribution here. This is not the place to rehearse the scandals of some of the baby formula companies or some of the pharmaceutical firms who have grossly overcharged for the active ingredients of drugs. Alan Berg concludes a careful survey of TNCs and nutrition by saying that, in spite of the substantial time and energy devoted by governments to involving big business, "There is little to show in the way

of nutrition improvement. Nor are the prospects bright
for reaching a significant portion of the needy with pro-
prietary foods marketed in the conventional manner. . . .
The major impediment is the inability to reconcile the
demand for corporate profit with a product low enough
in cost to reach the needy in large numbers."[5]

Insofar as appropriate products of a simple, not over-
specified kind, using local materials and local labor, have
not been invented, so that there are gaps in the product
range, there is clearly need for R & D. For the reasons
given, however, the TNC will not have the incentive to
devote its R & D to this purpose. For, having spent possibly substantial sums on an innovation, rapid imitation
will soon erode its profits, and it will not be able to recoup its expenditure. It is the very fact that the social
returns on such innovations exceed the private, appro-
priable returns, and that markets in developing countries
are more competitive, that leads to the minuscule research
that is done on appropriate basic-needs products. An example would be a cheap, say $50, refrigerator. The argu-
ment points to alternative methods of financing R & D.

Similar considerations apply to simple producer goods,
like hand tools and power-driven equipment, for both
small farmers and small industrial and service enterprises.
The appropriate technology may be missing or, though in
existence, may be unknown in the country. It is hard to
see, though, how the TNC could have an incentive to
spend funds on developing such products. There might
be more scope in supplying capital goods required as inputs into the public provision of basic services (road building equipment for geological surveys, medical equipment,
drugs).

Quite distinct and complex issues, not discussed here,
arise for the TNC and the host country in the area of
foreign trade. Labor-intensive manufacturing and agricultural production for exports provide opportunities for

employment, income generation, and the acquisition of skills, as well as tax revenue. On the other hand, excessive incentives in the form of tax concessions and subsidized inputs can lead to the phenomenon of "negative value added," just as it has in the more thoroughly studied case of high-cost import substitution. In both cases, profits to private foreign firms are consistent with social losses for the host country.

Technology

In spite of frequent charges that TNCs, compared with local firms, introduce excessively capital-intensive technologies into developing host countries, there is no evidence that *for the same product lines* TNCs use more inappropriate technology than local firms. Some evidence points to the opposite. The previous section argued that the real issue is not the technology for a given product, which at least within a range, is often dictated by the specifications of the product, but the product choice itself. Thus, the technology employed in a steel plant is largely determined by the degree of sophistication of the final products for which the steel is needed.

There has also been controversy on the location of the R & D activities, developing countries complaining that parent countries monopolize the bulk of this activity. However, R & D is a high-skill-intensive activity and this type of skill is even scarcer than capital in developing countries. Only where research depends on local conditions (as in much agricultural research on soil and climate) is there a strong case for the location of the research in the developing host country.

There is a clear need to devote substantially more R & D to the invention and dissemination of appropriate, capital-saving technologies and products, many of which have been identified. The difficulty, as already mentioned in the discussion of products, is that normally the TNC has no incentive to devote its resources to such research, because it does not offer the opportunity to recoup the full benefits derived from the expenditures through monopoly pricing.

Nevertheless, there might still exist an unrealized potential of TNCs for transferring and adapting existing technology and for inventing new and appropriate technologies. In order to reap maximum benefits, the developing countries would have to create the conditions for absorbing the contributions of the TNCs, possibly through joint ventures, conditions for training local counterparts, encouraging local research, and fostering attitudes favorable to such absorption.

But, as far as simple, basic-needs products and simple, capital-saving technologies adapted to local climatic and social conditions are concerned, there is no escape from the conclusion that it is in the nature of the TNC not to devote R & D funds to these purposes. The small, competitive local firms in the developing countries, on the other hand, do not have the market power and the means to embark on such research. The conclusion for policy again points to alternative ways of financing relevant R & D, either directly, through government finances, or indirectly, through government compensation for innovators, the social benefits of whose inventions exceed their private ability to appropriate returns.

TNCs and Small-Scale Local Enterprise

It is controversial whether TNCs encourage or discourage local entrepreneurship in the "informal" sector. Some observers have adduced evidence on subcontracting, showing the stimulating impact of TNCs; others have produced evidence that local intiative has been stifled. The two positions are, of course, not inconsistent for some types of activity might be encouraged, others discouraged. Government policies that have kept interest rates low and have rationed capital to large (including transnational) firms and that have discriminated in government procurement in favor of these firms have reduced employment, increased inequality, and run counter to a basic-needs approach. The complexity of government regulations, the encouragement of collective bargaining, minimum-wage legislation, and similar measures also make it more difficult for small-scale domestic firms to compete with the TNCs.

The Contribution of TNCs

It is sometimes said the TNCs passively adapt to the economic and political environment that governments create. Like the corner grocer, the TNC is said to respond to ruling prices and cater to existing demand. Such a picture flies in the face of mounting evidence. TNCs have actively attempted to shape their environment, from attempting to overthrow a legally elected government (ITT in Chile), to bribing a president to reduce export taxes in order to break a banana cartel (United Brands in Honduras), to bribing officials and royalty in order to sell aircraft (Lockheed, not a TNC, in a number of countries). Even if we rule out illegal, unethical, and improper activities, it is clear that TNCs attempt to influence governments when negotiating about establishing their subsidiaries or about the terms of the contract, including such items as tariff protection, labor laws, tax provisions, etc.

If their role in shaping the economic and political environment has been systematically underestimated, their role in contributing capital has been overestimated. As much as three-quarters of foreign investment by TNCs is now financed locally, either by retaining earnings or raising local capital. The special contribution of the TNC consists in the "package" of capital, technology, management, and marketing. One of the problems in assessing the impact of the TNC on BN is that some components of the package may have desirable, others detrimental, effects. The host country may not have the foreign marketing facilities that the TNC provides, but the TNC's technology may aggravate local unemployment. Or the company may provide skills for production for domestic consumption, but the product may be suited only for the upper-income groups. It is this fact, as well as more general cost considerations, that has led to the demand for "unbundling" the package and purchasing the missing components separately. But since the monopolistic strength of the TNC consists precisely in offering the whole package on a take-it-or-leave-it basis, it will be unwilling to agree to unbundling.

TNCs and Employment

A BN approach calls for raising the productivity and earning power of the poor. One of the most important ways of doing this is to increase remunerative employment opportunities. Can the TNCs make a contribution to job creation? On past evidence, the answer is not encouraging. Estimates of overseas assets by TNCs in the Third World are unreliable, but a plausible figure is that the stock of foreign capital in 1970 was $40 billion, of which half was located in Latin America and the Caribbean. This stock provided employment for approximately 2 million workers or roughly 0.3 percent of the labor force.[16] The average capital cost of creating a job is therefore $20,000. It appears that, on past performance, TNCs cannot make more than a negligible contribution to employment creation.

A BN-oriented approach, by spreading purchasing power more widely, would, of course, reduce the incentives to produce sophisticated products requiring capital-intensive techniques. A turn to a greater export orientation would enlarge the scope for labor-intensive export industries, particularly for the location of labor-intensive processes or the production of labor-intensive components by vertically integrated firms in developing countries. But here again, technical innovation may shift the comparative advantage if, as seems likely, mechanization can replace these labor-intensive processes.

In spite of some opportunities, the specific advantages of TNCs in a BN approach would be considerably smaller. There would be less demand for sophisticated, mass-produced consumer and producer goods. The scope for advertising and shaping tastes by sophisticated marketing techniques would be reduced. The profitability of R & D-intensive technology would fall. Both the need of host countries for TNCs and the incentive of these companies to operate in developing countries would decline.

Regional Integration

A BN approach, by attacking the prevailing dualism (in which a small privileged group has its links with the developed economies, while the rest remain in poverty), will tend to encourage intra–Third World trade. While at the moment the economies of the developing countries are largely competitive, there is considerable scope for complementarity and expanding trade. There is a tendency for the poor to consume the simple products that they themselves produce and for them to produce the products that they consume. There are clearly exceptions to this, and some basic-needs goods and services might well be appropriately produced in a highly sophisticated and/or capital-intensive manner. But, as a rule, a BN approach will tend to encourage intra–Third World trade, investment, and technical assistance.

Two distinct problems arise for the TNC. One is an anxiety shared by many countries. When several developing countries form a customs union, a free trade area, or a region of closer cooperation, new profit opportunities arise for the already operating and for newly entering foreign companies. Policies have to be devised to insure a fair sharing of these profits between the union and the foreign companies.

The historical legacy of communications, transport, credit facilities, and institutions will tend to reinforce the North-South connection, and the countries engaged in promoting collective self-reliance and regional cooperation may find it difficult to fit the TNCs into a pattern of South-South trade and investment. Changes in infrastructure, reductions of trade barriers, etc. may help, but historical and conventional North-South links may be hard to sever.

A second set of problems concerns the sharing of the gains from integration between different members of the union. The creation of a new form of international company, the shares of which would be held by the member countries of the union, might be one way of solving this problem, though it has so far not been successful. The proposal would be for the company to combine low-cost, efficient location and operation, not subject to political horse-trading, with a sharing of the gains between member countries.

Alternatively, there can be agreement on other forms of compensation, such as arrangements to pay higher prices for the exports of the less–industrialized member countries, to permit their citizens to migrate within the region, or to locate universities and research institutes in the less–developed partner countries.

Environment

In the new international division of labor which would be guided by differential pollution costs in different countries, the location of certain "dirty" processes in developing countries could be one of the functions of the transnational corporation, if the host countries are prepared to accept them. This could be done either by the firm locating dirty processes within its vertically integrated system of operations in a developing country where the social costs of pollution would be lower and the benefits from raising levels of living higher, or by transferring the whole operation to such a country. The argument would be analogous to that of locating unskilled or semiskilled labor-intensive processes and products in developing countries. One important point to be investigated here is whether the TNC cannot be used as a pressure group to insure access for these products to the markets of the developed countries, where protectionist pressures are disguised as a desire for environmental protection.

Bargaining

As the TNC has become one of the main vehicles of transferring modern, complex, and changing technology from developed to developing countries, an important aspect of policy consists of the terms on which the technology is transferred. In settling the bargain and in drawing up the contract, a large number of items may be negotiable. Some of these may refer to incentives, such as protecting the market for the product or improving the attractiveness of inputs (public utilities, a disciplined labor force, absence of red tape); others may lay down conditions for sharing the benefits with the host country, such as tax provisions, the use of local materials, local participation in management, training workers, creating jobs, raising exports, etc.; others again will relate to policies such as conditions about repatriation of capital and profits, raising local capital, etc. In this manner the consequences of the activities of the TNC can be tilted in the direction of meeting basic needs. Perhaps the most obvious instance is where the TNC itself makes no contribution to basic needs but the tax revenue collected by the government is used for financing rural public works, which improve the position of the rural poor.

In order to achieve such gains, skilled and informed bargaining is necessary. Hitherto, multilateral technical assistance in negotiations of this type and assistance in training negotiators has been on a very small scale. International organizations could render technical assistance in strengthening the bargaining power of developing countries in negotiating such contracts and contribute to an informed dialogue between managers of TNCs and public officials through training courses. What is needed is both direct technical assistance in drawing up contracts, possibly with the aid of a model contract, and indirect aid through training, providing information, and encouraging solidarity among developing countries to avoid competitive concessions.

Institutions

Another important area of policy is the imaginative exploration of new legal and business institutions which combine the considerable merits of the transnational corporation with the maximum beneficial impact on basic-needs satisfaction. This area comprises joint ventures, i.e., both between private and public capital and between domestic and foreign capital, which go further than window dressing by giving the developing host country access to information and decisionmaking and by making various provisions for divestment and gradual, agreed transfer of ownership and management from foreigners to the host country. Thus countries wishing to curb the power of large groups in their manufacturing sector may find investment reduced. This may make it advisable to institute a "joint sector" in which public capital is combined with private national management with or without an equity stake, or in which public capital is combined with private international capital. Another possibility would be a management contract with a national or international investor.

Thought and action in this area have suffered from a poverty of the institutional imagination, which has lagged behind the advance of the scientific and technological imagination. Discussions have turned partly on the ideological dispute between private and public enterprise. Yet the real issues have little to do with ownership. Mixed companies can be devised that simultaneously harness private energy and initiative yet are accountable to the public and carry out a social mandate, on the model of the British Commonwealth Development Corporation. Equally arid has been the dispute over the virtues and vices of private foreign investment. Here again, the task should be to identify the positive contributions of foreign firms and the social costs they impose on the host country, to see how the former can be maximized or the latter minimized, and to provide for gradual, agreed transfer to national or regional ownership and management. There is a need for a legal and institutional framework in which the BN objectives that are not part of the firm's objectives can be achieved while giving the firm an opportunity to earn profits by contributing efficient management and technology.

Finally, a basic-needs approach to development should explore the opportunities for a changed direction of the activities of TNCs. As we have seen, a basic-needs approach would enlarge the scope for intra-Third World trade and investment. New types of TNCs might emerge and should be encouraged. They might be smaller and more competitive. They might produce the simpler wage-goods and services required by BN, employ more labor-intensive technologies, and draw more on local materials.

They might make more use of local subcontracting, thereby encouraging local entrepreneurship and capital formation. TNCs have, in the past, shown great powers of adaptation. They have increasingly accepted host country conditions in the form of joint ventures, greater participation of local personnel, and even minority shareholdings. It might well be that their considerable flexibility will enable them to define a place for themselves in a BN approach to development.

IX. Toward a Country Typology

An important conclusion to be drawn from having identified the distinct features of a BN approach is the redirection of research. It is in the areas of the technology of public services, development administration, and development politics that future work is likely to yield promising results, although economists as such have little to contribute to some of the principal problems, except work on linkages and externalities. The work should start from an appropriate country typology that distinguishes: (1) between countries with relatively high average incomes per head, in which an emphasis on redistribution of income and assets and a redirection of social services can make a substantial contribution in meeting basic needs, and those with very low incomes, in which growth is an essential condition for meeting basic needs; (2) between countries whose political system encourages self-reliance and local mobilization and those that will depend heavily on external assistance; (3) between countries with high population density and little cultivable land, in which land redistribution holds out limited scope, and countries with abundant cultivable land in relation to their population; (4) between smaller countries that can hope for growth in employment opportunities from labor-intensive exports and larger countries, in which foreign trade plays a relatively smaller role; (5) between countries in which a large proportion of the population lives in the countryside and where rural development has greater importance, and those with a large proportion of urban population. Different political regimes and different administrative, technological, and ecological conditions are also relevant.

Work will also be needed on the development of systems of monitoring BN. Social indicators, methods of developing composite or integrated indicators (such as an extension of life expectancy to comprise the dimensions of basic needs), and their correlation with economic indicators are prerequisites for analysis and policy. Once these are available, we can assess the impact of policies on meeting basic needs.

NOTES

1. It may be thought that the notion "basic" precludes possibilities of conflict and trade-offs. But, since not all needs can be met at once, their hierarchy manifests itself as a succession in time. In the words of the *Dreigroschenoper:* "*Erst kommt das Fressen, dann kommt die Moral.*"

2. To the extent that meeting basic needs covers provision for the victims of disasters (floods, earthquakes, droughts) special arrangements are required and the argument of the text applies with less force.

3. Very low birth rates are registered in countries with low infant mortality rates and high life expectancy: Sri Lanka, China, Taiwan, South Korea.

4. Robert H. Cassen, "Population and Development: A Survey," *World Development* 4, nos. 10–11 (October–November, 1976). Cassen emphasizes the complex processes connecting these "correlates of fertility decline" and other aspects of development, including income and fertility. David Morawetz confirms statistically the link between BN and fertility decline. See "Basic Needs Policies and Population Growth," *World Development*, 6, nos. 11–12 (November–December, 1978).

5. A public opinion survey found that the majority of people

do not support general "welfare" programs, but at the same time do support specific measures, like helping poor families with deprived children. Similarly, "aid for development" is less appealing than help in meeting basic needs.

6. For evidence on this from Kerala, see *Poverty, Unemployment and Development Policy* (New York: United Nations, 1975).

7. P. V. Sukhatme, *Malnutrition and Poverty*, Ninth Lal Bahadur Shastri Memorial Lecture, January 29, 1977, Indian Agricultural Research Institute, New Delhi, p. 16.

8. Chapter II in Chenery et al., *Redistribution with Growth* (London: Oxford University Press, 1974).

9. A. K. Sen, "Poverty and Economic Development," Second Vikram Sarabhai Memorial Lecture, December 5, 1975.

10. Ibid.

11. For evidence that workers with more calories are more productive see an article by Christopher Bliss and Nicholas Stern, "Productivity, Wages and Nutrition," *Journal of Development Economics* 5, no. 4 (December 1978), pp. 331-98.

12. Abraham Maslow, *Motivation and Personality*, 2nd ed. (New York: Harper and Row, 1970), p. xiii.

13. Amilcar Herrera et al., *Catastrophe or New Society? A Latin American Model* (Buenos Aires: Bariloche Foundation, 1976), p. 51.

14. V. Nagam Aiya, *The Travancore State Manual*, vol. 2 (Trivandrum, 1966), p. 537.

15. Alan Berg, *The Nutrition Factor* (Washington: Brookings Institution, 1973), p. 158.

16. United Nations, *Multinational Corporations in World Development* (New York: United Nations, 1973).

An Age of Global Reconstruction

Celso Furtado

I. Development:
Theoretical and Conceptual Considerations

THE CONCEPT OF development, having originated in economics, where emphasis is laid on its quantitative aspects in the form of growth, inevitably goes beyond this context, penetrating into the domain of other social science disciplines, into cases where growth cannot be visualized as a homothetic process or cannot be understood in the absence of a system of values which the economist is unable to integrate into his conceptual frame. This ambiguity gives rise to a whole series of problems which have led economists to draw a distinction between development and growth, assigning to the first of these concepts, even when qualified by the adjective "economic," a breadth which perforce transforms it into an interdisciplinary subject.[1]

The sources of the notion of development may be detected in three currents of European thought in the eighteenth century. The first of these arises from the philosophy of the Enlightenment, with history being viewed as a gradual advance toward the supremacy of reason. The second is linked to the idea of the accumulation of wealth, in which it is taken for granted that the future holds out a promise of increased well-being. The third is related to the idea that the geographical spread of European civilization means access to superior modes of life for the other peoples of the world, considered as being more or less backward.

During the German Enlightenment in the eighteenth century, a philosophy of history—a secularized view of the development of society—emerged that took the form of a search for a "subject" whose essence is achieved through its own historical process. The faculties ascribed by Kant to the conscience of a transcendental subject constitute the starting point of an overall view of history: that of the transformation of chaos into rational order. With Hegel, mankind, as an entity which reproduces itself in accordance with a logic that aims in the direction of progress, assumes the role of the subject. This optimistic conception of the process of history, which allows a glimpse of the possible future in the form of a more productive and less alienating society where today's antinomies have been outstripped, leads to the quest for a propitious agent—the working class, the entrepreneur, the nation, the state—a "negativity" capable of sifting contradictions and precipitating the future, in other words, a vector of progress.

The publication of the *Critique of Pure Reason* was preceded by five years by that of the *Wealth of Nations*, which set out to prove that the pursuit of self-interest is the mainspring of the common good. The harmony Kant claimed to have discovered in the heterogeneous faculties of the human mind, in the form of "common sense," is seen in Adam Smith's social order to be the work of an "invisible hand." Adam Smith argues, however, that this harmony presupposes a certain amount of institutional order. The wealth appropriated by the feudal baron was of little value to the community, since it was spent on entertaining his commensals and was thus rendered unproductive. It is only in a society where obstacles to the flow of goods and to the exercise of individual initiative are reduced to a minimum that the harmony in question can come into being. Viewed thus, progress does not necessarily stem from the logic of history, but is within men's reach: the way to achieve it is known. The main point is to have institutions which enable the individual to develop his abilities to the full.

With mercantilism and colonialism, foreign trade was considered as an imperial activity, hence, inseparable from the power of the nations engaged in it. This doctrine came under fire from the middle of the eighteenth century onward and was gradually replaced by liberal ideas during the first half of the nineteenth century. International specialization made it possible to carry still further the division of labor, its positive effects on productivity being obvious in each country. According to the liberal doctrine, international trade leads to a better use of productive domestic resources, and the resulting increase in productivity is of benefit to all. A corollary of this doctrine was that, in forcing other countries to fall in with its lines of trade, Europe was performing a civilizing mission, thus helping to increase the welfare of peoples enslaved by obscurantist tradition.

Progress and Reality

While in the second half of the eighteenth century European thought was advancing on a number of different fronts toward an optimistic view of history—a view summed up in the idea of progress—contemporary social reality was by no means reassuring. The rise of commercial capitalism over the previous five hundred years had had relatively little effect on social organization. Agricultural products from a still feudal land-tenure system, articles manufactured by the guilds, and sometimes colonial products found their way into the commercial channels and strengthened the financial power of a bourgeoisie whose involvement in politics became daily more noticeable. Here the appropriation of the social surplus reflected the strong position of the bourgeoisie, which controlled trade channels vis-à-vis the land owners, the members of the trade guilds, and other subagents of production. A fundamental change took place when the traditional structures controlling production were dismantled (as in the case of the guilds) or reduced to the role of passive agents (landlords who became rentiers).

In this way the pattern of trade, previously based on an exchange of finished or semifinished products, became also vertical, a part of the structure of production with the elements or factors of production being converted into merchandise. Thus both land and labor gradually came to be regarded as commodities. This process, which led from commercial capitalism to industrial capitalism, had two main results. On the one hand, substantial new possibilities were opened up for the social division of labor, in the manufacturing sector in particular. Specialization at the level of the product or of an important stage in the production process was replaced by the division of work into simple tasks, which increased the possibility of using machines. On the other hand, the party with which the capitalist had to deal was no longer either an element in the dominant social structure or an entity with inalienable rights, but had become an isolated worker who could easily be replaced, given the simplicity of the task he performed.

The penetration of capitalism into the organization of production can be interpreted as a broadening of the social space governed by criteria of instrumental or formal rationality. The capitalist who had formerly dealt

with landowners, guilds invested with privileges, or similar
bodies, now had to deal with "production factors" which
could be regarded in the abstract, reduced to a common
denominator, and quantified. From this point onward the
sphere of economic activities could be considered apart
from other social activities. But the progress of "rationality" is neither more nor less than the widening of the area
of social relations governed by the criteria of mercantile
organization. The growing subordination of the vision of
the social process to the criteria of instrumental or formal
rationality brought about substantial changes in social
structures. In agriculture, for example, it led to the depopu-
lation of the countryside and the drift to towns or new
colonial settlements, sometimes on other continents. The
price revolution caused by more effective manufacturing
processes speeded up the decline of artisanal forms of
organization in areas where the conditions for creating
new types of employment did not exist.

Thus while the accumulation resulting from the progressive injection of market criteria into the organization of
production gathered speed, social structures entered a
phase of radical change. Some of the visible forms of this
change—the chaotic growth of towns, the disintegration of
community life, mass unemployment, the conversion of
human beings (including children) into merely a labor-
force—made contemporary observers deeply uneasy.[2]
This accounts for the pessimistic way in which the more
clear-sighted economists in the first half of the nineteenth
century viewed the future of capitalism, which appeared
to them to lead inexorably toward a stationary state. Their
central concern was the process whereby the social product
was appropriated and, indeed, how income was distributed.
Given the sharp rise in population which followed on the
rapid growth of towns, the "population principle" formulated by Malthus appeared to them to be obvious: any
increase in real wages would be canceled out by the popula-

tion growth generated thereby.[3] Again, the law of decreasing returns, which prevailed in agriculture, and the pressure to raise land rents, which accompanied agricultural expansion on poor-quality soil, combined to reduce investment potential, thus slowing down the capacity of the system to create employment. This idea of a trend toward long-term stagnation which, it was argued, could be deduced from the logic of capitalist economy was presented in different ways by classical economists and was to play a basic role in Marxist thinking. Marx, however, far from drawing pessimistic conclusions from this so-called trend of the capitalist system toward a loss of impetus, saw in it a clear indication that the "internal contradictions" of the system would inevitably grow worse. On Hegelian lines of thought, these contradictions can be presented as harbingers of a higher form of society in the making, one which will be more productive and less alienating. Thus, at a stage when the social cost of the process of accumulation was particularly high, criticism of capitalism directly contributed to maintaining the view inherited from the Enlightenment that such accumulation would open up the way to universal improvement.

Capitalist Stability and Technical Innovation

In identifying accumulation with a wages fund or, in other words, with a stock of current consumption goods ("corn," in the language of Ricardo) and in claiming that it could be measured in homogeneous units of simple labor, classical economists created considerable obstacles to an understanding of the part played by the development of technology in capitalist society. Technological progress came to be regarded as a means of economizing a scarce production factor (land, labor, or capital) which could be clearly defined in a microeconomic setting. This way of viewing technology, through the prism of an isolated productive unit, was at the root of the difficulties later encountered by economists in adopting a dynamic approach to economic processes rather than comparing static situations. A large number of the most significant forms of what is called technological progress—namely, economy in the use of nonrenewable resources, economies of scale, external economies, changes in the pattern of demand as a result of the introduction of new products, etc.—can be fully grasped only by an overall view of the social system and the nature of its relations both with the physical environment it controls and with the outside world.

Technological progress is a vague expression which, in the sense most commonly used, covers all the social changes which make it possible for the process of accumulation to continue, hence for capitalist society to reproduce itself. By "accumulating" is meant transferring to the future the ultimate use of resources available today. In capitalist society the action of accumulation brings in a return, with the result that the reproduction of social structures makes it necessary for accumulation to generate an increase in the overall productivity. But without changes in the availability of natural resources, in technology, or in the composition of final demand, accumulation inevitably tends toward a saturation point. Changes in the distribution of income on egalitarian lines may open up new outlets for accumulation but do not prevent a saturation point being reached. The same may be said of the discovery of better-quality or more abundant natural resources and also of the positive effects of opening up new channels for foreign trade. None of this alters the basic context, which is that of the trend toward diminishing returns as soon as there is overaccumulation. The group of factors which alters this basic context is what we call technological progress. This assumes visible form mainly in two ways: (a) greater efficiency of production processes and (b) the introduction of new end products.

Technological progress by means of the adoption of more efficient production methods, if unaccompanied by the introduction of new products, would not be sufficient for the accumulation process to continue without encountering major obstacles. After a certain stage accumulation could continue only if the labor force made use of it to a lesser degree or if social inequality were reduced. Moreover, accumulation based solely on the introduction of new products (without any change in the efficiency of production processes) entails growing social inequality. Briefly, the social changes implicit in the concept of development fall into two main groups: an increase in the efficiency of production techniques and a growing diversification of the final product. Let us consider what the social forces behind these two processes are, and what basic relationships exist between them.

When reproducing itself, capitalist society, which bears the seeds of the material civilization predominant almost everywhere today, generates a process of accumulation which tends to outstrip population growth. There is no need here to seek the historical reasons underlying this pattern of growth; it will suffice to recall what has been said about the social disorganization which occurred in the period when accumulation gathered speed and to refer to the position of strength of the countries which became industrialized when the system of the international division of labor was becoming established. Once a certain pattern had been set for the appropriation of the social product, the behavior of the ruling classes was directed toward their self-preservation, which meant that certain levels of accumulation had to be ensured.

This ineluctable rule of intense accumulation is the root cause of the instability which is characteristic of capitalist society. One must put down to the absence of any global theory of accumulation the fact that the science of economics, far from moving on toward an explanation of overall social processes, tended to restrict its field of observation, confining itself to studying the rationality of isolated agents. Neoclassical economists saw in the instability of capitalist society a reflex of adjustment to, or oscillation around, a position of equilibrium which could be strictly defined only by adopting as a postulate the absence of accumulation. The fact is that the perception of an economic situation, taken out of its overall social context, is possible only in a strictly synchronous analysis, that is to say, assuming that there is no real accumulation. Although Keynes remained true to the tradition of pure economics, he adopted an approach which was static only in appearance. His followers were not slow to understand that a congruence could only be obtained between the parametric role of the stock of capital and the flow of net investment by restricting the analysis to a consideration of situations of underemployment. At the macroeconomic level, net investment perforce signifies accumulation.

The models of growth which have been the subject of a major part of the theoretical work of economists in the last three decades are a by-product of attempts at a dynamic approach to the Keynesian model. The bulk of this work follows along two lines: on the one hand, renewed contact with the classical tradition, linked to a pattern of institutional distribution of income; and on the other, a continuation of the neoclassical tradition founded on the concept of the production function with flexible coefficients, linking the return on the factors with their respective marginal productivity. This theoretical work had only limited significance for the progress of ideas on development, both in the highly industrialized countries and in the so-called underdeveloped countries. The inability of growth models to account for major structural changes—i.e., the interplay between the "economic" and the "noneconomic"—and to record the com-

plex relations which arise at the boundaries of the economic system (the relations with other economic systems and with the ecosystem) stem from the very conception of the science of economics on which they are
based. The more sophisticated the model, the more remote it is from the multidimensional reality of society.
It was for this reason that the most important changes
—caused by the gathering speed of accumulation in the
last quarter-century and the advent of transnational
structures with an ever-growing role in the allocation
of resources, the creation of liquidity, and the geographical distribution of income—have taken place without the theorists of growth having grasped their impact at the level of national economic systems. The
inability at present shown by the governments of the
great capitalist nations to reconcile the aims of their
respective economic policies is in great part due to the
direction taken by the theory of growth and to its
considerable influence on the elaboration of these economic policies.

While it is true that the reproduction of capitalist society generates a substantial potential for accumulation,
it is also true that such accumulation can be achieved
only through delicate and continuing alterations to social
structures. It is thus necessary to consider how the reproduction of structures of privilege succeeds historically in
blending with the need for change. The ruling classes,
who control the strategic points in the decisionmaking
system, direct their policies toward preserving the privileged position they occupy. In so doing, however, they
trigger a large-scale process of accumulation which gives
rise to a demand for labor in excess of population growth
and promotes social tensions. While in the early stages—
when artisanal structures were being dismantled—accumulation proceeded under conditions of an elastic supply of
labor, in time it came up against a growing inelasticity of

supply, necessitating population movements, mobilizing the potential of female labor, etc. The reproduction of a capitalist economy is inconceivable without such social tensions, which have been resolved by directing techno- logical progress so as to offset any rigidity in the labor supply. Those who claim to have discovered in the logic of capitalism an inexorable trend toward stagnation, the aggravation of social antagonisms, and self-destruction, underestimate the potentialities of technology for gener- ating new power resources. The agents who direct or supervise economic activities in capitalist society seldom form part of a system having objectives explicitly estab- lished beforehand. In reality such agents compete for po- sition, triggering off a process of accumulation which pro- duces pressure to increase the share of labor in the social product. Thus in competing with each other these agents unleash forces which are conducive to reducing the space for which they are competing. This situation favors agents who innovate with a view to economizing labor.

Social antinomies and the constant outstripping of the tensions resulting therefrom generate the sweeping social changes which characterize the development of capitalism. On the one hand, substantial accumulation and, on the other, the concentration of economic activity are condu- cive to making the individual worker an element in struc- tured social groupings, thereby giving rise to new forms of power: all of which tends to transfer social conflicts to the political level. Thus the driving force specific to capitalist society is above all a result of the fact that the reproduction of its built-in structures is based on techni- cal innovation. In other words, the advance of technology is given every facility to succeed by this society, precisely because it ensures the perpetuation of the privileges of the ruling classes. However, the assimilation of technologi- cal progress in a competitive society implies substantial accumulation, which in turn generates social pressures for a reduction of inequality. Thus the combined action of technological innovation and accumulation makes it possible for the privileges to continue and to exist side by side with the social forces which challenge them.

So long as a capitalist economy succeeds in continuing to grow, the expectations of agents with antagonistic interests can be satisfactorily met: real wages increase, and the share of capitalists and other privileged groups in the social product tends to be maintained. A superficial observer would see only a field of class conflicts and antagonism between members of the same class. Since accumulation and the penetration of technological progress bring about continual changes in relative prices, speed up the installation of new equipment to replace that which has become outdated, continually eliminate certain goods from the market, alter the distribution of income both in space and in time, and concentrate economic power, etc., the field is extraordinarily unstable, and appears, from a certain angle, even to be chaotic. But from a wider viewpoint it can be seen that it is thanks to this mutability (in which Marx claimed to have discovered anarchy) that capitalist society reproduces itself and maintains its basic class structure.

The Criteria of Development

The concept of development has been used in two cases with reference to contemporary history. The first concerns the evolution of a social system of production which, by means of accumulation and technological progress, becomes more efficient, that is, increases the productivity of its labor force as a whole. Concepts such as "efficiency" and "productivity" are, of course, ambiguous when applied to complex production systems in which inputs and outputs are heterogeneous and vary with time. It can, however, be admitted as self-evident that the social division of labor increases efficiency of manpower—and that accumulation is not only a transfer in time of the ultimate utilization of a resource but also the means whereby the division of labor takes on a diachronic dimension. The possibility of intensifying the division of labor is considerably increased when tasks which are carried out simultaneously are supplemented or replaced by others which can be spread out over periods of varying duration. The worker who uses a tool shares the work with others who previously contributed, directly or indirectly, toward making the tool concerned.

The second case in which reference is made to the concept of development relates to the degree to which human wants are satisfied. In this case the ambiguity is even greater. There is a first level at which objective criteria can be used: the satisfaction of basic human needs such as food, clothing, and housing. The life expectancy of the population—bearing in mind certain distortions due to social stratification—is an indicator of the degree of satisfaction of basic needs. As we move away from this first level, reference to a system of values becomes proportionately more urgent, since the very idea of a need when unrelated to essentials becomes obscure outside the cultural context to which it belongs.

The concept of development can accordingly be approached on the basis of three criteria which have a complex interrelationship: the criterion of an increase in the efficiency of the production system; that of the satisfaction of the population's basic needs; and that of the attainment of the objectives linked to the use of scarce resources, sought by various groups in a society, The third criterion is certainly the most difficult to define, because what represents well-being for one social group may seem a mere waste of resources to another. That is why the view of development held by a society is not unrelated to its social structure.

An increase in the efficiency of production—commonly

defined as the main indicator of development—is not an adequate prerequisite for the fuller satisfaction of the population's basic needs.[4] We cannot rule out the possibility that the deterioration in the living conditions of the population at large is due to the introduction of more efficient technique. Furthermore, an increase in the availability of resources and a rise in living standards may occur in the absence of any change in the production process when, for example, the pressure on reserves of nonrenewable resources is increased. The current view of development overlooks the fact that in the capitalist system the creation of economic values entails a greater cost than that which is shown in either private or public accounting systems. Man's productive activity increasingly involves irreversible natural processes such as dissipation of energy, which tend to increase universal entropy.[5] The stimulation of forms of technology based on a growing use of energy (the outcome of the short-term view engendered by the private appropriation of nonrenewable resources) aggravates this trend, making of the economic process something which makes increasing inroads on resources as time goes on.

In the process of the reproduction of capitalist society, technological progress fulfills a dual role: it reduces the pressure for social equality and it keeps consumption by middle- and high-level income groups growing. Thus the orientation of technological progress governs the evolution of the entire production system, the structure of which must be such as to ensure the social diffusion of products originally reserved for high-income minorities. For example, the mechanization of the individual transport of high-income minorities and the subsequent search for economies of scale in the production of automobiles lead to the spread of the habit of using the same kind of transport among the general public, even though this entails substantial social costs.

The subordination of technological creativity to the

objective of reproducing a social structure which is largely nonegalitarian and where accumulation is at a high level is the root cause of some of the most paradoxical aspects of contemporary civilization. Even in countries where the accumulation process is the most advanced, a proportion of the population (between one-tenth and one-third) has not reached the level of real income required to satisfy what are regarded as basic needs. Cases occur in which an increase in wages is part and parcel of a process which includes both an increase in the coefficient of waste inherent in expenditure by high-income groups and the spreading throughout middle-income groups of more and more sophisticated forms of consumption. Thus the elimination of "poverty in the midst of plenty" may become more difficult as accumulation proceeds. Now it is precisely in terms of the values of this civilization that an awareness has been born of increasing inequalities in living standards among nations, of accumulated backwardness, of *underdevelopment*. And it is with reference to the problems involved in international inequalities that the concept of development has grown up as a central concern in this time.

The geographical concentration of economic activities for the benefit of a small number of countries was one of the most striking consequences of the intensification of the accumulation process. Adam Smith had already observed that the opportunities created for the social division of labor are much greater in manufacturing than in agriculture.[6] The division of work into tasks in manufacturing subsequently opened up unprecedented possibilities for accumulation and gradually changed the structure of manufacturing, in that the separation between production processes tended to prevail upon product specialization. Thus the interdependence of manufacturing activities began to increase both synchronously and diachronously. As industrialization proceeded, the idea of productivity, which could be grasped at the microeconomic level in agriculture and handicrafts, gradually became inseparable, from the degree of development attained by industrial activities as a whole. In addition, since technological innovation—both in production processes and in the composition of the final product—is conducive to the appropriation of the surplus by those in its vanguard, it is easy to see that in a capitalist economy a structural tendency exists toward a concentration of income which benefits urban areas (where manufacturing activities are grouped together) and countries exporting products which incorporate the most sophisticated technology.

That these problems were recognized is shown clearly in the great debate which took place in the second half of the nineteenth century on free trade versus protectionism. The reaction against the doctrine of free trade was based on the idea of the complementarity of economic activities and was to lead to the concept of the national economic system. The spread of industrialization, which produced in the second half of the last century a whole constellation of independent economic centers, took place for the most part in the context of national protectionism. From then onward the concept of development became clearly bound up with the idea of national interest.

The Rise of Structuralism and Dependency Theory

From the end of World War II onward, reflection on development had, as its starting point, awareness of the economic backwardness of certain countries in relation to others, assessed by the differences between levels of productivity and/or consumption. Other indicators of a social nature were soon added, such as infant mortality, the incidence of contagious diseases, the degree of literacy, etc., thus contributing to the confusion of the concepts of "development," "progress," "social welfare," and "modernization," all seen as giving access to lifestyles created by industrial civilization.

This reflection began by taking the form of a political concern, which was the fruit of the major changes brought about by World War II, such as the dismantling of colonial structures and the appearance of new forms of dominant international interests based on the mastery of technology and ideological manipulation. During this first stage a major catalytic role fell to the new international institutions—the United Nations, its regional commissions and specialized agencies—whose secretariats carried out the first empirical studies with a view to defining these new problems.

The fact is that for the last three decades reflection on development has remained directly related to problems in which the political dimension has been decisive: the deterioration in the terms of foreign trade, the fact that the price system was ill suited for use in orienting investment, the insufficiency of accumulation in societies exposed to the demonstration effect, the inadequacy of traditional institutions when faced with the new functions of the state, the unsuitability of imported technology for coping with the potential supply of factors and the dimensions of the domestic market, outdated agrarian structures, the tendency for income to be concentrated, structural tensions reflected in chronic inflation, continuing disequilibrium in the balance of payments, and so on. This complex group of questions was broached without any appropriate attempt at theorizing in advance and almost always in a totally inadequate conceptual context.

With its primary emphasis on an overall view of economic decisions where inadequate coordination was responsible for unemployment, the work of Keynes gave great impetus to the theory of economic policy.[7] Keynes's analysis gave rise to a theory of the coordination of economic decisions which set considerable store on decision-making centers at the national level. But if the elimination of unemployment required action by the state in directing the economic system as a whole, what about the structural modifications essential in order to overcome underdevelopment? This approach led to emphasis being laid on the political aspects of economic problems and to the concept of development as the fruit of deliberate action, not the effect of natural evolution.

In taking an overall approach to economic problems, development specialists are led to resume contact with the tradition of historicist thought which contributed to the criticism leveled against international liberalism in the middle of the nineteenth century. With neoclassicism, the theory of production was limited to an abstract study of the individual enterprise and its cost equation in a context which was regarded as neutral. But the social antinomies inherent in capitalism, which are inseparable from the driving force behind it, cannot be apprehended from a study of isolated agents. The first step toward formulating a theory of production is not taken until one has grasped the interdependence of productive activities, which makes it necessary to start with the idea of a system. The historicist tradition had produced, with Friedrich List, the concept of a system of productive forces which was to be used extensively by Marx.[8] This concept shed light on the complementarity of productive activities, which are regarded as a social process not as an aggregate of isolated entities. In this way external economies, which are of considerable importance in the study of development, can be included in the theory of production. Thus the inadequacy of microeconomic criteria of rationality for defining a model of social productivity becomes obvious.

Possibly no concept has had so much significance for the advance of studies on development as Raúl Prebisch's concept of the center-periphery structure.[9] Though Prebisch's main concern was the international propagation of the business cycle—the diversity of behavior of economies which export primary products by comparison with economies which export industrial products—the concept was based on an overall view of the capitalist system and opened the way to a perception of its structural diversity, a knowledge of which is essential in order to understand the special character of underdevelopment. The elaboration of this concept by Prebisch himself and by the group of social scientists which met at ECLA (The United Nations Economic Commission for Latin America)—a group known as the Latin American structuralist school—gave rise to a trend of thought which has had considerable influence.[10]

Prebisch's starting point was a criticism of the system of the international division of labor and the theory of international trade based on the concept of comparative advantage, the validity of which was still uncontested in the academic world. One of the corollaries of this theory was that international trade not only provided an "engine of growth"—it enabled all participating countries to make more rational use of their own resources—but was also a factor in reducing inequalities in living standards between countries, since it eliminated some of the negative effects brought about by the lack of complementarity of the available factors. Yet the empirical data on the long-term behaviour of prices in international markets by no means confirmed these forecasts. Such evidence as existed was the other way around, i.e., it pointed toward the concentration of income in the hands of countries having the highest level of income. Prebisch brought the problem out of the abstract context of theorems of comparative advantage (an exercise in logic in which the conclusions are implicit in the premises) into the context of social structures within which costs are worked out and surpluses appropriated. The difficulty of bringing down money wages in industrial economies was pointed out by Keynes, who ascribed it to the vigor of trade-unionism. But the situation was different in countries which exported primary products, a theme which was shortly to be linked to the theory of the structural surplus of labor. Thus there is a structural tendency in the capitalist system toward concentrating income to benefit of countries which have a more advanced form of social organization. Disparities in the rate of accumulation, due in part to the system of the international division of labor and its impact on social structures, have produced a structural heterogeneity in the capitalist system which cannot be ignored in any study of international relations. Thus underdevelopment came to be regarded not as a stage on the road to development, but as a permanent structural feature.

Another idea of considerable importance brought to the fore by the Latin American school in the early 1950s was that of the harmful effects of the types of technology incorporated in equipment imported by late-developing countries.[11] Bearing in mind the fact that these types of technology are bound up with prevailing social relationships in countries with advanced accumulation, it is easy to understand why it causes an ever-increasing concentration of income in countries where accumulation is in its early stages and frequently creates an incompatibility between the maximum profits sought by private enterprises and the social objectives of development policies. This subject subsequently aroused considerable interest with the debate on urban marginality, the choice of techniques, labor-intensive techniques, technological dependence, etc. The work of the Latin American structuralists evolved toward an interdisciplinary approach to underdevelopment, considered as corresponding to a type of society in which the relations of external dependence that are interjected into the structure of the society influence the reproduction of the society itself.[12]

An Overview of Development Thinking

Let us try to sum up. The process whereby the world economic system was formed had from the outset two quite separate aspects. The first relates to radical changes in production methods, i.e., the destruction, in whole or in part, of family, artisanal, feudal, and guild forms of organization of production and the gradual establishment of markets for production factors, such as labor and the natural resources appropriated by man. These radical changes resulted in greater opportunities for the division of labor and technological progress, which explains the heightened pace of accumulation.

The second aspect relates to the upsurge of commercial activities, i.e., the interregional and international division of labor. The regions in which accumulation first began to gather speed tended to specialize in activities for which the contemporary revolution in production methods had opened up greater possibilities for the progress of technology and became centers which generated technological progress. However, geographical specialization also brought about increased productivity, that is to say, a more efficient use of available resources. These increases in productivity, the results of foreign trade, acted as vectors which transmitted the innovations of the material culture reflecting the acceleration of accumulation. Progress—the assimilation of the new life styles produced by innovation in the dominant culture—became the universal ideology. The modernization of models of consumption—the imitation and adaptation of large fragments of the material culture—was able to make substantial progress without markedly interfering with social structures, which explains how in many parts of the world foreign trade was activated in the context of preexisting forms of the organization of production, including slavery.

The dissemination of capitalism was much swifter and more widespread as a modernization process than as a process of bringing about relevant changes in production methods and social structures.[13] Development and underdevelopment are thus historical processes which stem

from the same initial impetus, i.e., they have their roots
in the acceleration of accumulation which took place in
Europe at the end of the eighteenth and the beginning
of the nineteenth century. For an understanding of the
causes of the historical persistence of underdevelopment,
it is necessary to observe it as part of a whole which is
in movement, as an expression of the driving force behind
the world economic system produced by industrial capitalism.

The industrialization of countries which have been
caught up in the underdevelopment trap takes place in
competition with imports, not with artisanal activity.
It thus tends to be subordinated to the modernization
which precedes it. Far from being a reflection of the
level of accumulation reached, the evolution of the production system is a simple process of adaptation in which
the dominant role falls to the external and internal forces
which determine the profile of demand. This is the basic
reason why the social structures of countries with belated
industrialization are so different from those which arose
in areas where industrial capitalism developed as an independent process.

The mechanization of infrastructures and the transformation of agriculture, provoked by the drive to export
and by developing trends in internal demand, together
with the impact of industrialization in cases where artisanal activities were important—for example in sectors
such as food, textiles, and clothing—set in motion a long-
drawn-out process of destruction of traditional employment structures. The tremendous and chaotic spread of
towns, to be found in all underdeveloped countries, is
only one of the most visible signs of this complex process of disintegration of social structures. The concept
of disguised unemployment, introduced by economists
in the early 1950s, was the first form of an awareness
of this problem; but it was the studies on urban marginality

carried out in the subsequent decade by Latin American sociologists which made it possible to apprehend it in all its complexity and to bring out the special character of the social structures in countries with dependent economies.

Populations deprived of their traditional occupations by changes in the forms of production tend to move into urban cultural subsystems which have only sporadic links with markets but have a strong potential influence on them as reserves of labor. Marginalized populations, which are largely independent in reproducing themselves, are an expression of a type of social stratification which has its roots in modernization: The technological mismatch referred to by economists has been reflected, from the sociological point of view, in the two extremes of modernization and marginalization. The attempt to find common theoretical ground leads to the theory of dependence, which is based on an overall view of capitalism as an expanding economic system and aims at apprehending the heterogeneity, in time and space, of the process of accumulation.

These studies, which bring out the basic links between the external relations and the internal forms of social domination in countries which have been caught up in underdevelopment, have highlighted other subjects of equal importance, such as the nature of the state in these countries and the role of transnational corporations in controlling their economies.

Where modernization has been based on the exploitation of nonrenewable resources (the case of the oil-exporting countries, though an extreme one, lends itself most easily to analysis), the surplus kept by the country of origin tends to be taken over by a central system of power. In this way links with the outside world come to play a basic part in the evolution of the power structure, leading to its centralization and reinforcement. This process, coinciding with the disintegration of social structures, confers on the state characteristics which are only now beginning to be recognized as unique. As the state is primarily an instrument which appropriates the surplus, the evolution of social structures tends to be strongly influenced by the way in which the state directs the utilization of the resources it controls. It is thus in a country's relations with the outside world and in the process of accumulation that we find the bases of the power system whose action intervenes in that restructuring of society which accompanies the spreading out of capitalism.

The situation of countries which are linked with the outside world through the exploitation of nonrenewable resources and in which the state is the primary, almost the sole, instrument of accumulation controlled from within is obviously an extreme case. However, in other underdeveloped countries political trends are moving in the same direction: the strengthening of the state machinery is the general rule, as is the emergence of new forms of social organization under its guardianship. Investments in infrastructure and basic industries depend directly on the public authorities or on the guarantees given by them to foreign groups. Local saving, to a large extent compulsory, would not exist without deliberate action by the state, which assumes growing responsibilities in the production field itself, where the enterprises it establishes operate with a considerable margin of independence. In the face of these trends it is no longer possible to apply traditional criteria to differentiate government activities from private ones. That is why Weber's concept of bureaucracy linked with the forms of power that are based solely on instrumental rationality is of little value in accounting for the new realities of power to which we are referring.

The study of development, by leading to a gradual rapprochement of the theory of accumulation with the theory of social stratification and the theory of power, finds its place at a strategic point where the various social science disciplines converge. Early ideas on economic development, defined as an increase in the flow of goods and services which was more rapid than population growth, have been gradually replaced by others which are linked to a complex of social changes that acquire meaning with reference to an implicit or explicit system of values. Measuring a flow of goods and services is an operation which has specific meaning only when such goods and services are related to the satisfaction of objectively defined human needs, that is to say, needs which can be identified independently of existing social inequalities. Ambiguity will, however, always exist in any attempt to reduce to a common denominator expenditures by the different groups of a nonegalitarian society, or in any attempt to compare increases or reductions in inequalities. The postulate of the homogeneity of consumption expenditures is incompatible with the idea of social welfare, which, in one way or another, is included in the concept of development, since the hypothesis of an egalitarian society is excluded. The controversy on this point—apparently only a technical one—has led to a criticism of the types of society implicit in development projects.

It is easy to see why this controversy arose originally in underdeveloped countries, since the type of society in question already exists on account of these countries' backwardness and dependence. Thus, the type of traditional thinking about obstacles to development seemed likely to be replaced by another type, which fed the controversy on the limits of growth, development styles, types of society, and world order. An in-depth analysis of the international relations of domination and dependence and their effect on social structures has given a

clearer insight into the nature of the forces which insure
the permanence of underdevelopment. In addition, criticism of the "logic of markets" has thrown light on the
impact on the ecosystem of a type of society which encourages accumulation at the same time that it inevitably
reproduces inequalities.

The fruitfulness of the critical reflection stimulated by
the theory of development is most certainly due to its
interdisciplinary nature, and the horizons it has opened
up may well have contributed to the enrichment of man's
view of the contemporary world.

II. Center-Periphery Relations
in an Age of Global Reconstruction

The System in Its Current Phase

The most significant structural trait of the capitalist
system in its current phase seems to be the center-periphery
discontinuity. All attempts to consider the current dynamics of the capitalist system should start from this
basic fact, as disparities between center and periphery
are becoming increasingly accentuated. Growth in the
center of the system takes place with a social diffusion
of its fruits, whereas in the periphery it takes place with
income concentration. But, since the periphery pays the
center for the technology it utilizes and since part of the
surplus generated in the periphery is appropriated by
central enterprises, there is a permanent flow of resources
from periphery to center, which means that, under normal circumstances, income tends to get concentrated in
the center. In fact there occurs a double process of income concentration: within the system as a whole it
benefits central countries, and within each peripheral
country it benefits the minority which reproduces the

lifestyle generated at the center. When growth at the center is accelerated, implying an intensification of the flow of innovations at the level of consumption goods, the repercussions in the periphery are twofold: increased income concentration and a relative increase of accumulation out of the system of production.

Approximate data available at present indicate that the average annual growth rate (namely productivity or per capita income) for the 1948–1970 period was 3.5 percent in the center and 2.5 percent in the periphery. In 1970 the average income in the center was something on the order of 10 times as large as average income in the periphery; the average increase in the consumption of a citizen in the center over a one-year period was 14 times as large as that of a person in the periphery.[14] In 1970 the center population was about 800 million people, in contrast to 1700 million people in the periphery. In addition, by virtue of differences in demographic growth rates, the center population increased by nearly 8 million in 1970, while the periphery population increased by over 40 million people.

The second important characteristic of contemporary capitalism is the tendency toward integration of central economies under the leadership of the transnational corporations. This process largely accounts for the acceleration of economic growth; indeed, the growth rate in the last quarter-century was twice as large as growth rates in any other 25-year period since the beginning of the Industrial Revolution. The acceleration of growth in the center accentuates structural tendencies, such as an increased gap between center and periphery, and income concentration within the peripheral countries. Thus the fundamental aspect to be kept in mind for an understanding of the present dynamics of the system as a whole is this process of integration, which presupposes the existence of a power structure able to create the conditions necessary for the big, transnationally operating companies to expand. Such a power structure was a consequence of World War II, from which resulted the unification of the security systems of capitalist countries under U.S. tutelage. Thus a mutation at the political level which occurred three decades ago opened the way for a complete reshaping of the world economic framework. From the political mutation emerged the ideology of interdependence, of solidarity with former enemies, of abolition of the old colonialism, of equal opportunities for all enterprises of large and small countries, and of access of all central countries to the high consumption standards that had been developed in the United States. The institutionalization of this power structure remains in an embryonic stage, although the creation of regional instances, especially in Europe, has permitted certain advances toward a better coordination of decisions on economic matters.

That the institutionalization of the overall power structure remains an open process is an important datum, for the tensions generated by the accceleration of growth seem to be reaching a critical stage at present. Surprising as it may seem, it does seem clear that the greatest hindrances to progress in this area have come from the United States. The acceleration of growth in this country fostered the implantation in other countries of branches of big U.S. enterprises. However, the transnationalization of a given enterprise leads to the creation of a flow of resources from branches into headquarters. When such branches are located in underdeveloped countries, the necessity to equip and provide them with high-level technology inputs allows the creation of an inverse flow of American exports, especially if the subsystem is expanding. The solution is not simple when branches are implanted in other central countries. In fact, the development of the American economy in the last decades shows a trend to an overproportional growth of imports, which makes the goal of full employment even harder to achieve in the United States than in other central countries. At first sight the problem seems to be a simple consequence of overvaluation of the dollar. But we must consider that, at present, the most rapidly expanding sectors of the American economy are the branches of American enterprises abroad and that those brances have three-fourths of their operations financed by local resources and are using local cheap labor to produce for the international market, including the U.S. market. As a consequence, a structural tendency has been created to increase importations into this country. To seek to correct such trends by means of simple monetary devaluations (which stimulate exports) would mean to accept a progressive degradation in terms of trade. Because of the considerable difference in labor costs, many American enterprises are restructuring themselves by running their productive activities in the periphery with the U.S. market in mind. As a result of such structural changes, the American economy has been forced to accept a level of chronic unemployment that is two or three times as high as that of the other central countries. An important area of conflict thus appeared between vast sectors of the American population and the interests of the rapidly expanding transnational corporations. The fact that the Nixon administration, while Congress was pressing toward adjournment, hastened to obtain a trade law in order to carry on the effort toward external liberalization indicates the existence of apprehensions and uncertainties for the future but also demonstrates the intent to carry on with the process of global integration of the capitalist system in spite of domestic tensions. The hypothesis of a partial return to protectionism is not excluded, especially if chronic unemployment becomes worse; but it would be erroneous to suppose that a partial withdrawal of the United States toward protectionism would necessarily mean a change in the course of development in the long run.

In the remaining central countries the process of transnational integration has contributed to a considerable
strengthening of local enterprises, whose expansion abroad
opens the way for economies of scale from which the population as a whole benefits. Even the implantation of branches
of American companies in those countries is contributing
to the substitution of imports and to the creation of new
export lines. The end result therefore has been the inverse
of that observed in the United States: increased competi-
tiveness and dynamism in the export sector with positive
effects on employment levels. The concern of the European countries to strengthen big enterprises abroad is a
clear indication that the process of integration will continue. However, as big enterprises become more and more
autonomous due to their growth outside of national
boundaries and their alliances with other big enterprises
in joint ventures in several countries, their relationships
with the state in their countries of origin take on new
characteristics. It is commonplace knowledge that the
state seeks to act at the international level in the interests of the big corporations of its country. But in domestic politics the state tends to represent the interests
of broader social groups. The instability that has been
generated in the international system and propagated
to the national economies that have to choose between
inflation and stagnation will necessarily have repercussions on the political level and may lead national governments to take up greater responsibilities at the social
level. In other words, if the trend toward autonomy for
big corporations continues, it is conceivable that the
state will assume increasing functions at the social and
cultural level, with more concern for ends—the style of
development, quality of life, etc., than for means—organization of production, financing of accumulation, etc. If
the big corporation tends to operate as a transnational
institution within the capitalist system, the defense of

employment levels and the preservation of the social and cultural interests of the present national societies will probably become the main concern of national states. It would therefore be expected that such states will become more and more controlled by socially oriented political parties, that is, parties which effectively represent the bulk of the working population.

The relationships between central national states (individually or as a group) and the political superstructure of an increasingly integrated capitalist system will surely be influenced by the internal institutional development of the United States. If unemployment becomes more serious in the United States and if a partial return to protectionism occurs, it is conceivable that the internationalist sector now under leadership of the big oil companies will seek to buttress its alliances abroad, thereby providing an opportunity for other large states in the capitalist world to increase their role in the controlling institutions. The success of the Rabouillet-type conferences confirmed this tendency. It is in the light of these possibilities that consideration must be given to the prospects of the formation of a political bloc in Western Europe on the basis of the institutions which emerge from the Rome Treaty. Once the possibility of Europe being equipped with an autonomous defense system and world strategic capabilities is exluded—the unification of Europe along these lines would face serious obstacles posed not only by the United States but by the Soviet Union as well—it is to be recognized that the international role of a loosely united Europe would not be very distinct from the role of a reasonably structured European Economic Community. In order for European enterprises to achieve the stature of their American counterparts, a strong concentration of capital would be necessary, and it would almost certainly be to the benefit of German enterprises. In practice, this would not happen without obvious resistance. On the other hand, big American corporations are largely established in Europe and would benefit equally with or more than local enterprises in the case of increased unification. In a politically united Europe, it would not be easy for France to maintain the level of defense autonomy that it currently enjoys, and there is little doubt that in the political sphere the relations between Europe and the United States would be closer to the current German line than to the French. The fact is that the formation of the European Economic Community benefited the big enterprises established in the various countries and favored the expansion of big American firms in Europe. Therefore, the EEC should be seen as a fundamental datum in the process of integration of central economies and not as the formation of a European economic system in opposition to the American system. A unified center for political decisions in Europe would not guarantee a stronger European presence in the control of the capitalist system, for such a center would necessarily be fragile.

The Emergent Structure of Power

If we examine the global picture just described, we may perceive distinct action plans, or areas of "power condensation." First, there is the political superstructure, which is little institutionalized and which originated under American tutelage. There are a number of factors that provide the political structure with consistency and relative stability: evidence that the capitalist system does have boundaries within this planet and that an important part of those boundaries is quite fluid in the periphery; the particular political charter of two large industrial nations (West Germany and Japan) resulting from the way the last world war ended; the enormous costs to the United States of mounting and constantly renovating the unified security system. However, the need to maintain this superstructure at a low level of institutionalization indicates that power distribution within the system remains an open process. Thus the crucial goals at the superstructure level should not be confused with the specific interests of any one national subsystem. It would be naive to think that such specificity of the superstructure derives from a balance of power among the principal nations in the capitalist world or from an imposition of American designs. It expresses the fact that the global power structure is still in its formative stages. One of the most important elements of such a power structure is the network of the transnational corporations.

The second level of power condensation consists of the national states of the center. The situation of the American state is obviously unique by virtue of its double function at national and international levels. What is important to stress in connection with the national states operating in the center of the capitalist system is the growing responsibilities of such institutions in the defense of the welfare of populations. The defense of domestic employment levels (threatened by instability waves generated in the international sphere) and the necessity to preserve or improve the quality of life tend to be very high on the list of political concerns in the so-called postindustrial societies. There is room, therefore, for a perfecting of the political life with an enlargement of the representativeness of the decision centers. It is as if the alienation of power to the supernational institutions and to the big enterprises had increased the social responsibility of central states, since the state is the only institution at this level which exerts a *legitimate* power, i.e., a power that embodies explicit values and which has been effectively delegated by a population.

The third level of power concentration corresponds to

peripheral national states. Here the heterogeneity—economic as well as social—is greater than that observed at the center of the system. What is important to stress is the generalized emergence of the techno-bureaucratic power and the decline of the traditional dependent bourgeoisies formed in the framework of the system of the international division of labor. While these latter had structural solidarity with metropolitan centers, the techno-bureaucratic power emerged as an agent which seks to maximize its own independence. Obviously this power does not emerge in a vacuum. Nearly always it appears as an extension of some traditional locus of power—managers of the interests of international groups, watchdogs for a local oligarchy, etc.; then it experiences an expansion of its functions in times of crisis and establishes itself as an arbitrator when new contenders appear in the struggle for power. Where problems of negotiation with big transnational enterprises appeared, the techno-bureaucratic power found the conditions for rapidly establishing itself and taking up the role of guardian of the national interests. The need to decode the information manipulated by the big enterprises increased the value of so-called technicians and created new sources of social prestige. In other places, the new financial and industrial functions of the state would lead to similar results. What is common to the manifestations of the techno-bureaucratic power in the periphery is the fact that it tends to be in confrontation with the transnational corporations and is guided by the intent to share a part of the surplus which they appropriate locally. Fiscal, monetary, credit, and commercial instruments are used to reach this objective. In more recent times, direct control has been exerted over part of the capital of local subsidiaries of the big enterprises.

The fourth level of power crystallization consists of

the big enterprises which operate transnationally. Those are the main instruments for accumulation, for technical innovations, and for the integration of the system. In the periphery, exploitation of nonrenewable resources and industrialization take place under direct control or with ample participation of these enterprises, and this provides them with considerable power vis-à-vis their own governments. Enterprises which operate in the framework of oligopolies are essentially oriented by the idea of growth and, since the easiest way of growing is to operate simultaneously in various markets—a given innovation may be simultaneously exploited in several central countries, and equipment which has become obsolete in a high-wage country may be transferred to another country where labor is less expensive—they constitute the real moving force for the global integration of the system. In this way, as interdependence or integration increases, the participation of big enterprises in the generation of employment and appropriation of surplus also increases. The effective autonomy, as sources of technology and centers manipulating financial resources, of transnational corporations constitutes the most important feature of contemporary capitalism. Economic decisions in the framework of the old national economic systems were coordinated by criteria of complementarity and by creation of external economies and self-sufficiency in regard to the supply of basic products. Such criteria do not prevail for a transnationally organized enterprise. This explains the considerable relative increase in oil consumption, the dramatic expansion of oil imports in this country, the abandonment of alternative energy sources, and the orientation of technology toward an acceleration of the consumption of nonrenewable resources. Having appropriated oil reserves located in peripheral countries at extremely low costs, the big enterprises proceeded to maximize short-term advantages without worrying about effects on consumer and producer countries. There is no doubt that intensification of economic growth necessarily leads to an increasing interdependence between countries and regions within the capitalist system. But we cannot ignore the fact that if the interests of the multinational corporations prevail, such a process tends to speed up, creating a serious dependency of the majority of central countries on the periphery as far as the supply of nonrenewable resources is concerned. Another important consequence of the prevailing rationality of the transnational corporations manifests itself in the geographic localization of manufacturing activities. Within the framework of a central national economy, labor costs and the purchasing power of the population are two aspects of the same process. Since productivity increases unequally in the various sectors of activity, if the average wage rate increases with average productivity (which does happen in central countries) it is because relative prices are modified so as to benefit those sectors where productivity increases are slower. The framework in which a transnationally expanding firm operates is fundamentally different, for in this case there is no relationship between labor costs and the purchasing power of thsoe who will acquire the produced goods.

The New Center-Periphery Relations

The growing dependency of central countries on nonrenewable resources that originate in the periphery is a fundamental datum for the understanding of the present tensions in the capitalist system. As far as oil is concerned, two observations need to be made. The dramatic increase in oil consumption in the central countries prevented the formation of a real inter-dependency, that is, the producing countries could not prepare themselves to absorb their share of the surplus which has given them increased freedom of operation. Even the suspension of exports during a relatively important period would not create insurmountable difficulties to the more important exporting countries. From this point of view, the oil-producing countries are different from the other countries that export raw materials. This is the only explanation for the relative rapidity with which they reached an agreement to manage prices in the international market. The second point to be considered is of a different sort; it refers to the U.S. dependency (beginning in the late 1960s) on Middle East oil, a fact which has undeniable political implications. This point became clear in October 1973 when Middle East oil was used as a convenient political weapon against the U.S. government. Until then it was taken for granted that the existence of a strategic reserve of basic raw materials combined with local production and the diversity of reliable external sources would protect the U.S. government from this type of situation. This freedom of action explains why, up to quite recently, the pressures generated within the country by conflicting interests did not interfere too much with increasing responsibilities assumed at the international level by the U.S. government. The oil embargo demonstrated that certain types of international action can no longer be carried out without a domestic support broader than was necessary, for example, for involvement in the Vietnam War.

The aggravation of tensions within the capitalist system since 1970 has two main causes, namely, the slow pace of the process of institutionalization at the level of the superstructure and the changes in power relations between central and peripheral states. The form in which the extended frontier war of Vietnam was conducted and the particularities of the prolonged Middle East conflict—for which in the United States the foreign policy aspects cannot be separated from the domestic aspects—eroded the American leadership and certainly retarded the institutionalization of the superstructure, permitting the initiative for reshaping the international order to be passed to the peripheral countries.

If we add to this the debilitation of the executive branch in the U.S. government (in view of the increasing difficulties in reconciling the interests of the big enterprises engaged in the global integration of the capitalist system with the increasing awareness of population groups concerning the negative aspects of such a policy), it is understandable that the government of this country had to face increasing difficulties to pursue a coherent policy. Energy self-sufficiency would mean a substantial increase in energy costs, which would further reduce the competitive power of the American economy and foster investment of American firms abroad. Since the big American enterprises are engaged in the global expansion of the system, energy self-sufficiency is not interesting to them. The surplus transfer caused by the abrupt rise in oil prices meant in fact an increase in the investment potential of the system as a whole, which cannot but benefit big American enterprises. The development of other energy sources is certainly imperative, since oil is a nonrenewable resource. But this will not prevent dependency on foreign oil sources from continuing to increase.

Moreover, such dependency is not limited to oil. According to U.S. government estimates, dependency on foreign sources of strategic mineral products is also growing inexorably. Of the thirteen minerals considered to be strategic, only four (nickel, manganese, tin, and bauxite) were over 50 percent dependent on importation in 1970. By the end of this century, this degree of dependency will probably extend to all of the thirteen minerals on the list, with a dependency of more than 80 percent predicted for seven of them.

Once the hypothesis of a return to the status quo ante is excluded, the necessity is created for a reshaping of the power structure to allow a more effective participation of the other large central states with some form of representation of the peripheral countries. Awareness of such a necessity is behind the discussions concerning the reshaping of the so-called international economic order. Relationships between central and peripheral states have to be adapted to the new situation, given the increasing importance within the capitalist system of primary resources (nonrenewable resources and manpower) available in the periphery.

The circumstances surrounding the abrupt rise in oil prices in 1973 contributed to dramatize this aspect of the process of integration of the capitalist economy. But the intensification of growth and the preeminence of big enterprises in the decisionmaking process would necessarily lead to a growing utilization of the periphery's primary resources. On the other hand, the elimination of the remains of the old colonialism and changes in the social base of the peripheral state will necessarily lead to greater local retention of the surplus generated by exports. The 1946 legislation by which the government of Venezuela established state rights to half of the profits in the oil business constituted a historical milestone in center-periphery relationships. Since big oil companies traditionally administer prices on an international scale (crude oil is largely sold to refineries of the same enterprise), it was not difficult to assimilate taxes paid to production costs, transfer profits into transport and refining activities, and reestablish the profit margin at the expense of the consumers. Thus an implicit agreement was established between oil-producing countries and the big enterprises operating in this field. As the former company cartel was replaced by a state cartel, the conditions appeared for an ample international transfer of resources.

However, even if we disregard the exceptional situation of some oil-exporting countries, we should recognize that the prevailing tendency in a growing international economy is toward a valorization of the primary resources of the periphery, especially nonrenewable ones. Protection of a resource such as manpower—by means of international agreements between peripheral countries that could secure a modicum of remuneration (including local taxes) to workers in export industries controlled by transnational corporations—is a remote goal. But there is little doubt that this is the direction of the development of center-periphery relations. Since the transfer of resources that we have been discussing takes the form of changes in the terms of trade between center and periphery to the advantage of the latter, the volume and value of international transactions tend necessarily to increase. In the readjustment phase where the growth rate of exports from center to periphery has to be greater than the growth rate of exports from periphery to center, inflationary pressures in the center have to increase, as seems to be happening. It is natural that, faced with this situation, the governments of several central countries affected by the transfer of resources resort to measures which necessarily incur increases in domestic unemployment levels. However, it would be a mistake to assume that such situations forecast a cumulative unemployment process out of control, although this does not protect certain industries from experiencing increased difficulties by virtue of the deceleration of growth and the change in the composition of expenditures. This is the case of the auto industry in Europe, for example, which suffered the strong impact of the increase in the relative prices of oil at a moment when regional markets approached the saturation point. Since the expansion of auto companies in the periphery—an expansion which is accelerated by the transfer of resources—is assuming the form of the establishment of progressively integrated subsidiaries, the global growth of these enterprises may coincide with a reduction of their activities in their original countries. In any case, the effects of the deceleration of growth are not so strong in the sectors which directly benefit from increased exports to the periphery: production of capital goods, equipment, engineering services, management, etc.

Search for a New Civilization Project

The above-mentioned transfer of resources is only one aspect of a more general problem, namely, the increasing relative scarcity of nonrenewable resources and the responsibility of big enterprises in the predatory use of such resources. Insofar as the big enterprises are responsible for the general orientation of the development process, the use of nonrenewable resources tends to be thought of in a short time perspective. On the other hand, the big enterprises' power in the capitalist system is large, involving the generation of savings, orientation of technical innovations, and manipulation of consumers. Such power enables them to frame the reproduction of the economic-social system in such a way as to avoid significant modifications in the distribution of income, preserving their own share, This type of economic development has been characterized by increasing costs in terms of nonrenewable resources. Since there is a tendency for new models of products to become widespread due to the demonstration effect. we witness the establishment of an irreversible process of increase of the waste coefficient in terms of nonrenewable resources. Consideration of the problem of orientation of development and quality of life will probably lead to a confrontation between the state and the big enterprises in central countries. Since the easiest and socially most acceptable way to reduce the waste coefficient consists in changing the patterns of consumption, favoring the satisfaction of collective needs, the trend is toward steering income distribution and reducing the big corporations' power over innovative activities directly associated with the formation of consumption patterns.

As far as the periphery is concerned, the growing power of the big corporations is an even bigger problem. As we have already noted, the orientation of the industrialization process by these enterprises implies the transplantation into peripheral countries of ways of life that are appropriate for countries on a much higher level of accumulation. It should be added that such ways of life imply a considerable waste of scarce resources, a waste which is boasted of by privileged minorities alongside the misery of the bulk of the population. However, by some perverse effect, the valorization of nonrenewable resources has negative repercussions in many parts of the periphery, which is quite heterogeneous. The present tensions which cause transfer of resources from center to periphery also aggravate disparities within the latter. Here it would be important to distinguish among three situations. First, there is a small group of oil-exporting countries which, due to their reduced populations, will probably reach the degree of social homogeneity and income levels of central capitalist countries. A second and demographically much more important group of countries, formed by nations that export oil and/or other primary resources, may be able to benefit from changes in terms of trade and experience a persistent increase in their growth rates. However, because of the orientation given to the development process—industrialization under the control of subsidiaries of transnational corporations— such increases in growth rates tend to aggravate social inequalities. A third group of countries imports oil and other nonrenewable resources; this group is the weakest link in the whole system. It is on this group of countries that pressures generated by the degradation of the terms of trade coverage at present, as well as pressures arising from income concentration which is inherent to peripheral capitalism.

There seems to be no doubt that the present structural tendencies of the capitalist system lead to an increase in social unrest in the great majority of peripheral countries, either as a consequence of degradation of the terms of trade (as in the case of the third group of countries mentioned above) or as a result of improvement of the terms of trade through an intensification of growth and increased concentration of income (as in the case of the second group). Given the increasing versatility in many peripheral countries of the techno-bureaucratic power, which is always ready to rearrange its social supporting base, movements are emering that have programs of social reconstruction as their goal. Such movements lead to changes in the relationships with big corporations everywhere, no longer just in terms of appropriation of a greater part of the surplus, but also in terms of reducing their action as determining forces in molding the way of life of the population. A tendency is apparent to approach development from the standpoint of an identification of the fundamental needs of the population and a mobilization of the latter toward taking responsibility for many tasks from which it benefits directly. Thus economic activity tends to become explicitly subordinated to a social project.

In summary, the most significant structural tendencies manifested in both the center and periphery of the capitalist system seem to favor the subordination of economic criteria to social values. It would be naive to suppose that the time of growing disparities between center and periphery is coming to an end. But there are signs that a period of convergence toward a conception of development which implies a new civilization project is in the making.

III. Reshaping the International Economic Order

The only apparent unanimity reached during the last moments of the Seventh Special Session of the United

Nations General Assembly, the easy consensus achieved
by the large capitalist powers at Rambouillet, and the
difficulties which surfaced in the so-called North-South
conferences are all clear indications that the rich countries
still hold the initiative in the process of readjustment,
presently in course, of the power structure which influences international and transnational economic activities.
It is appropriate, therefore, to wonder if the poor countries will attain the objectives which they intended when
they decided to take the debate regarding the reconstruction of the international economic order to the public
arena, a debate which was previously limited to groups
of experts.

A real reform of that order implies attacking two types
of problems: those related to the coordination and control
of transnational corporations' activities, particularly the
creation of liquidity and short-term transfers of financial
assets; and those related to structural factors which generate the concentration of income in favor of rich countries and which are responsible for the aggravation of the
inequality of standards of living among countries. Rich
countries long insisted upon dealing solely with problems
of the first type. Poor countries, since the 1973 OPEC
victory, have demanded a broad and bold approach to
problems of the second type. Even though it is not possible to speak of objectives explicitly shared by all of
these countries, a certain consensus has emerged from
the long discussions in various international fora, from
which it is possible to attempt the elaboration of a coherent doctrine. The following points constitute a minimum agenda inspired by that doctrine.

Need to Reformulate the Supervisory Structure
of International and Transnational Activities

The present structure, created at the Bretton Woods
(1944) and Havana (1948) conferences, is rigidly supervised

by the United States. An effective reformulation of the present decisionmaking system requires different forms of coalition among the peripheral countries. The large majority of these countries have less than 5 million inhabitants and are technologically and financially incapable of controlling and utilizing the flow of information that feeds the international decisions system. It is not a matter of limiting the individuality of countries or asking them to abandon the effective defense of their interests, but rather of creating intermediate instances where problems common to the countries of a region or to a type of activity can be discussed and objectives defined. A regional grouping may include subgroupings, just as participation in a functional group (e.g., petroleum exporters) does not exclude participation in other functional groups (e.g., exporters of iron ore, copper and bauxite). What is important is that, in the confrontation with central countries, the most significant groups of peripheral countries can, when necessary, rapidly reach common decisions. The ultimate objective would be to have the power of veto every time any of the fundamental problems of the Third World is in play.

Need to Raise the Value of Labor in the Periphery

The value of labor varies from country to country according to the average amount of capital allocated per laborer. As the accumulation of capital in the capitalistic system is concentrated in certain areas (the central countries), the wage rates vary enormously among countries independently of the physical characteristics of the produce of labor. Thus a worker in an electronics plant located in a Third World country may earn less than one-tenth of the amount earned by a worker doing the same job in a central country, even if both are employees of the same firm, use the same technology, and produce for the same market. According to the current theory of international trade, the products originating in the peripheral country should be sold at a lower price, which would drive competitors out of the market. But in practice this rarely happens, for the TNC finds it convenient to "administer" the price of the product in question so as not to create problems in high-wage countries, appropriating the surplus resulting from the low wages of the periphery.

And what about products not produced in large consumer markets, such as tropical products? The theory of international specialization explains that it is good business for Brazil to produce coffee but teaches us very little about the price at which coffee should be sold on the international market. The parameters for measuring the advantage of producing coffee are the living conditions of the rural worker in the subsistence economy: the average productivity of the Brazilian economy increases when a worker is transferred from the subsistence economy to a coffee plantation. But nothing prevents adding another parameter to isolate the international price of coffee from the influence of the low standard of living of the Brazilian rural population. When Brazil provided two-thirds of the international supply of coffee, the government tried with some success to administer the price by regulating the supply. Similar practices were later adopted by various governments, not only to protect the real income of farmers vis-à-vis other economic groups of the country but also to protect the country against international speculators. The raw materials agreements of recent times are a milder version (a compromise between producers and consumers) of these attempts to organize the markets.

Even the most orthodox economist knows that in the so-called imperfect markets, rents are created in favor of this or that group of agents. In agricultural markets the asymmetry is obvious, for the demand is, in general, much more concentrated than the supply. In a world economic

order which aims to eliminate the exploitation of one
people by another, the parameter for determining the
price of supply in international markets of products such
as coffee or cocoa should be the average value of labor
in all producer and consumer countries of the product
in question. Let us admit that in capitalist economies
the value of labor corresponds to the average income of
the population. As the average income of the Third World
population is between 20 and 25 percent of the average
income in the whole capitalist system, it is easy to see
how far we have to go to attain a more just world economic order. We are not speaking of redistributing income
in the sense of transferring to poor countries resources
that are in effect the fruits of labor of the population
of rich countries, even though there are many justifica-
tions for a transfer of this kind. We refer solely to the
labor that is incorporated into products that circulate internationally, to which it is appropriate to recognize a
value corresponding to the average productivity of the
economies that participate in those transactions. As that
productivity increases, the parameter used to measure
the value of labor would have to rise. Neither do we suggest the establishment of rigid prices but rather a control
of fluctuations of these prices and recognition of a minimum value of the labor whose fruits are internationally
shared. It is true that a policy of this kind might simply
result in the creation of labor aristocracies in some Third
World countries. Its implementation, therefore, should be
accompanied by other measures to assure an adequate
use of the resources produced by the increase of real
income. Such a policy demands gradual implementation, for transfers of income, both within and among
countries, entail secondary consequences difficult to
foresee.

In the price formation of mineral products, the cost of
labor directly employed is of little importance. But a non-

renewable resource should not be spent without regard
for the consequences for future generations. The fact that
these resources can be exploited on the basis of criteria
strictly reflecting the interests of private individuals surely
constitutes one of the most serious shortcomings of our
civilization. In the sixteenth century, the kings of Castille
empowered Francisco Pizarro to conquer the Inca Empire
and decide according to his own interests what to do with
its dignitaries and wealth. Innumerable objects of gold,
noble expressions of one of the world's great cultures,
were melted down to be more easily transported and
sold. A similar situation has existed with respect to the
exploitation of nonrenewable resources: corporations
whose only motive is profit obtain permission from local
authorities, often by manipulation, to exploit this or that
nonrenewable resource as quickly as possible. Until very
recently, petroleum was exploited in the Middle East with
token payments to local authorities scarcely free from imperialist domination. And this irresponsible exploitation
occurred not only in dominated countries. In the United
States also a narrow privatist conception of the problem
has resulted in the destruction of an immense inheritance,
with grave consequences that are only now beginning to
be perceived. This privatist criterion in the exploitation
of nonrenewable resources greatly influences the direction
of technological progress, contributing more than any
other factor to the transformation of our civilization into
an infernal machine generating irreversible processes of
degradation of the physical world. One measure to change
this is to set minimum prices for nonrenewable resources
along the lines that the U.S. government proposed for oil.
This minimum price would be the starting point for a
gradual future elevation, destined to reorient technology
toward greater economies in the use of such resources.
This future increase could take the form of a tax destined
to help the poorest peoples.

*Need to Direct the Creation of International Liquidity
to the Solution of the Most Urgent Problems of Mankind*

That the United States should hold almost exclusively the
privilege of creating international liquidity constitutes one
of the most damnable aspects of the present economic order.
There is no doubt that the resource transfers resulting from
the exercise of this privilege occur mainly among the rich
countries whose central banks accumulate large reserves of
dollars. Furthermore, these transfers are to a certain degree
inevitable, given the imbalance of international transactions.
The problem raised is one of regulating the creation of international liquidity, controlling the actions of speculators
in order to reduce the foci of instability, and orienting the
resources released by the creation of means of payment
toward the solution of the most urgent problems, which
are those of the poorest peoples.

*Need to Break Up the Industrial System Concentration
for the Benefit of the Third World*

This objective also responds to the interests of the rich
countries, worried by the problems created by pollution
and by the necessity of housing a growing number of socially unintegrated foreign laborers. If industrial activity
is displaced toward countries where labor is abundant, the
present direction of technological progress, in the sense of
increasing the amount of capital per worker, can change.
Maybe more than any other, this factor would counteract
the tendency to the concentration of income mentioned
and also reduce the pressure on nonrenewable resources.
But this displacement must be conceived as part of a global
policy that also takes into account the need to increase the
value of labor in the Third World. For the time being it is
being carried out as a project of TNCs which find it an additional source of surplus. Placing the labor of one develop-

ing country in competition with another, TNCs are following the same policy they followed in the past with respect
to the exploitation of the reserves of nonrenewable resources of those countries. Furthermore, the entrance of
TNCs into the industrial sector necessarily brings a rapid
modernization of manufacturing activities linked to the
local market, control of these activities by foreign interests,
and the aggravation of the social inequalities. These negative aspects of present tendencies must not inhibit us from
seeing the heart of the problem. If an increase in the value
of labor is prompted in Third World countries—which does
not mean raising the wages and salaries of a small fraction
of the labor force, but rather the appropriation by the
community of a larger part of the surplus created by transnational activities—industrial displacement will constitute
a decisive factor in reducing social, as well as international,
inequalities and will also bring effective benefits to the
peoples of presently superindustrialized countries.

Need to Change the Development Style

This objective includes the former ones and represents
something more than their simple sum total. There is no
doubt that the lifestyle now prevailing in the center of
the capitalist system is not within reach of the people of
the Third World countries. The myth of economic development, i.e., the millenium which promised to all the peoples
of the world access to the lifestyles of today's rich societies, is already a thing of the past. The periphery will
never be a copy of the center. The accumulation of capital and technological progress will necessarily create in
Third World countries either a much more egalitarian or
a much more inegalitarian society than that which exists
today in central countries. We can be sure that history
opens to the people of the Third World the possibility
of living in societies more just than those existing at present

in countries that have reached the peak of abundance. But we can also be sure that the tendencies of the present world economic order operate relentlessly to worsen social inequalities in the Third World. Awareness of this reality, illustrated by the immense waste of scarce resources which results from the emulation of the lifestyles of rich countries by the privileged minorities in the poor countries, constitutes one of the causes of the demand for a new international economic order. To change the development style toward a more egalitarian society in Third World countries involves planning consumption before rationalizing production, i.e., giving priority to the ends rather than the means. There is little doubt that change in this direction depends essentially on the social forces acting within each country. But it would be a grave error to ignore the fact that this change can be thwarted by actions of external forces, especially since TNCs are the principal beneficiaries of a continuation of present tendencies. What is expected from a new international economic order is the creation of conditions allowing people to exercise their options without undue external pressures and to receive external aid whenever the effort of social reconstruction has negative economic repercussions in the short and medium term. It is an open question whether or not Third World countries will be successful in their present efforts to modify the world economic order. But on one point there can be no doubt: The persistence of present tendencies in the direction of growing inequalities constitutes an accumulation of destabilizing forces which tend to change, in an unforeseeable way, the course of our civilization.

NOTES

1. An extensive bibliography on theories of economic growth is to be found in F. H. Hahn and C. O. Mathews, "The Theory of Economic Growth: A Survey," in *Surveys of Economic Theory* (London: Macmillan, 1965). For a more selective bibliography, see the introduction by Amartya Sen to *Growth Economics* (New York: Penguin, 1970). The bibliographies available on theories of economic development are less comprehensive. See the select bibliographies listed by Benjamin Higgins in *Economic Development* (New York: Norton, 1968); Charles K. Wilber in *The Political Economy of Development and Underdevelopment* (New York: Random House, 1973) and Henry Bernstein in *Underdevelopment and Development* (New York: Penguin, 1973).

2. Sismonde de Sismondi, who described the beginning of the introduction of criteria of "rationality" into agricultural activities in Italy and England, has handed down to us an invaluable account of the impression made on his contemporaries by the subordination of the social process to economic criteria. See his *Nouveau principles d'économie politique* (Paris: Calmann-Levy, 1973), first published in 1819.

3. In this way there was ascribed to a biological law what in reality were the external signs of the transformation which had taken place in the system of social domination.

4. It is only in relation to the satisfaction of basic needs (which can be defined objectively) that one can speak of measuring the efficiency of a society's production system.

5. In this connection, see the work of the pioneering Georgescu-Roegen, *The Entropy Law and the Economic Process* (Cambridge, Mass.: Harvard University Press, 1971).

6. Cf. Adam Smith, *The Wealth of Nations*, ed. Edwin Cannan (Chicago: University of Chicago Press, 1966), vol. 1, p. 7.

7. The first edition of the work of J. M. Keynes, *The General Theory of Employment, Interest and Money* (New York: Harcourt Brace and World, 1964), came out in 1936. The first attempt to make the Keynesian model dynamic was by R. F. Harrod, in "An Essay in Dynamic Theory," *Economic Journal*, March 1939, pp. 14–33.

8. Cf. Friedrich List, *Das nationale System der Politischen Oekonomie* (Tübingen: Mohr, 1959), first published in 1841.

9. The ideas of Raúl Prebisch were presented for the first time in *El desarollo económico de la América-latina y algunos de sus problemas* (Santiago: United Nations Economic Commission for Latin America [ECLA], 1949).

10. A number of aspects of Latin American structuralist thought and a bibliographical guide are presented by Celso Furtado in

Economic Development of Latin America, 2nd ed. (New York: Cambridge University Press, 1976).

11. The first approach to the problem of the relationship between imported technology and underdevelopment is to be found in the study prepared by the ECLA team in 1951, *Theoretical and Practical Problems of Economic Growth* (Santiago: United Nations Economic Commission for Latin America, 1951).

12. For a sociological presentation of ideas on dependence see F. H. Cardoso, "Les Etats-Unis et la théorie de la dépendance," *Revue du Tiers Monde*, October-December 1976, pp. 805–825. See also Celso Furtado, *Théorie du développement économique*, 2nd ed. (Paris: P.U.F., 1976).

13. On the general subject of modernization, although it is approached from other angles, see S. Eisenstadt, *Modernization: Protest and Change* (Englewood Cliffs, N.J.: Prentice-Hall, 1966); and Marion J. Levy, Jr., *Modernization and the Structure of Society: A Setting for International Affairs* (Princeton, N.J.: Princeton University Press, 1966).

14. Cf. United Nations Economic Commission for Latin America, *Economic Survey of Latin America*, 1971, vol. 1, table 2; see also press release of the World Bank, no. 38, September 1971.

Economic Development:

A Marxist View

John G. Gurley

DEVELOPMENT ECONOMISTS OFTEN speak of three worlds. In many of these analyses, the First World comprises the advanced capitalist countries, the Second the Marxian socialist countries, and the Third all the rest—that is, the non-Marxian less-developed countries, or LDCs. I intend to look, through Marxist eyes, at the recent experience of economic development in the second and third groups and to assess that experience.[1]

I begin with an account of how the three worlds came into being and what their recent growth experience has been. I then turn to the development performances of the Third World countries, including in those performances not only growth rates of GNP but equity and other considerations as well. The next section contains an evaluation of this development experience and the lessons to be learned from it. I next survey the development performances of the socialist countries, especially China and the USSR. A reassessment of this analysis and my conclusions follow.

Throughout this article I write not only as a Marxist but also as one who is interested in sharpening Marxian analysis in this area. My criticisms of Marxian studies are meant to be friendly and constructive.

I. The Evolution and Present Features
of the Three Worlds

In the early years of this century there was essentially one world, a capitalist one, that was divided into a few wealthy colonialist countries and many oppressed, impoverished ones. At that time several industrial capitalist nations, led by Great Britain, controlled most of the world and had designs on the rest of it. Africa, weakened from centuries of the slave trade, was almost completely carved up—a third belonging to Britain, a third to France, and a third to Belgium, Italy, Portugal, Germany, and Spain. The Middle East, extending to the Persian Gulf, was in the dominion of Britain and France. India and Burma were parts of the British empire, as were Ceylon and Malaya. The French were the conquerors of Indochina, the Dutch the masters of what is now Indonesia. Several powers had territorial claims in China, and the United States, Britain, and others, with guns, goods, and investments, dominated and profited greatly in South America; and U.S. hegemony was taking shape in the Caribbean and Central America. In addition to parts of the empire just mentioned, the British domain also comprised Australia, New Zealand, Canada, Newfoundland, and South Africa; the partially self-supporting areas of Malta, Jamaica, Bermuda, and the Bahamas; the crown colonies of Hong Kong, Trinidad, Fiji, Gibraltar, and St. Helena; and other territories. Russia, a backward capitalist country, controlled an empire extending to the Pacific Ocean, but some of its own resources were in the hands of France, Britain, and others. Finally, Japan, a rising capitalist power, was carving an empire out of Korea, Manchuria, and other vulnerable areas.

That was the world on the eve of the First World War, when Germany, a late arrival to colonial ambitions, challenged the British and French empires. Within a few years, this war among the leading capitalist nations set the stage for the Bolshevik revolution. This worker-peasant uprising of 1917 was the first successful Marxist assault on the capitalist citadel. A few years later, Mongolia became the second Marxist state. Then two decades went by with no further breaching of the bourgeois ramparts. However, in the wake of the Second World War—which was largely Germany's renewed challenge, joined by the rising imperialist aspirations of Italy and Japan—eight eastern European countries and the northern part of Korea became Marxian socialist and, perhaps the biggest event of all, the Chinese Communist revolution succeeded at about the same time. Since then, Marxism has spread to Cuba, Vietnam, Laos, Cambodia, Angola, Mozambique, Guinea-Bissau, PDR of Yemen, and perhaps to three or four other countries (Benin, Ethiopia, Guyana, part of the Palestinian movement, Chile for a while). In addition, Marxism has recently gained some ground in France, Italy, Portugal, and Spain; it is still a force in India, Japan, Chile, and Greece; and the mountains and forests of the world, not to mention the sand dunes, conceal many Marxist guerrilla movements.[2]

At the present time, then, there is a Marxian socialist world and a capitalist world. The latter, as I noted above, is often divided into the advanced (industrial) capitalist nations and the non-Marxian less-developed countries, the First and Third worlds.

The advanced capitalist countries produce two-thirds of the world's GNP, but they have only a quarter of the world's land area and only a fifth of the world's population. Down below, at the other end, the Third World countries are in quite the opposite situation. They produce a mere 13 percent of global GNP, but they have almost half of both land area and population of the world. The Marxian socialist countries, comprising the Second World, lie in between. They produce a fifth of global GNP and have about a third of both land area and population.

One consequence of these relations is that the people in the advanced capitalist countries have a (weighted) GNP per capita of around $5,000, while those in the Marxist nations have less than 20 percent of that living standard and the people of the Third World less than 10 percent.[3]

There are, however, a scattering of wealthy countries within the Third World, notably several of the OPEC members, such as the United Arab Emirates, Kuwait, and Qatar. When the 13 OPEC countries are separated from the rest of the Third World, the non-OPEC group is revealed to be much impoverished, having a (weighted) GNP per capita of only 7 percent of the level enjoyed by the advanced capitalist countries (see Table 1).

During the period 1960–1974, the annual growth rate of GNP in each of the three worlds was roughly the same. But because the growth rate of population was relatively low in the advanced capitalist countries, somewhat higher in the Marxian socialist group, and quite high in the Third World, the advance of GNP per capita was rapid in the wealthier capitalist nations, less so in the Marxist group, and dismayingly slow in the LDCs as a whole, but especially in the non–OPEC Third World countries (see Table 2).

II. Recent Growth Experience of the Third World

The non–OPEC Third World expanded its GNP per capita during 1960–1974 by something less than 3 percent per annum, which is certainly not bad by historical standards. But about three dozen of these countries, which had over half the population of the group, had at best 1½ percent growth and at worst a negative growth. On the average, these laggards just barely made it across the zero line, which means that this group as a whole, with its almost 900 million people—dominated by India's 600 million—more or less stagnated in per capita terms during this long period.

TABLE 1

GNP, POPULATION, GNP PER CAPITA, AND LAND AREA IN THE "THREE WORLDS," 1974

Country Grouping	GNP (in 1974 US $ billions)	Population (in millions)	GNP Per Capita[a] (in 1974 US $) Weighted	Unweighted	Land Area (thousands of sq. miles)
Advanced Capitalist (25)	3,635 (66%)	731 (19%)	4,973	4,672	12,547 (24%)
Marxian Socialist (24)	1,167 (21%)	1,322 (34%)	883	983	15,487 (30%)
Third World (140)[b]	734 (13%)	1,838 (47%)	399	1,033	24,388 (46%)
OPEC (13)	184 (3%)	292 (7%)	631	3,349	5,065 (10%)
Rest of Third World (127)	550 (10%)	1,546 (40%)	356	796	19,323 (36%)
Total or Average	5,536	3,891	1,423	1,508	52,422

Source: *World Bank Atlas*, 1976.

[a] The weights are by population

[b] These are non-Marxian less-developed countries, including trusts and territories.

TABLE 2

ANNUAL GROWTH RATES OF GNP, POPULATION, AND GNP PER CAPITA, UNWEIGHTED, 1960-1974

Country Grouping	GNP	Population	GNP Per Capita
Advanced Capitalist (25)	5.23	1.07	4.16
Marxian Socialist (13)[a]	5.01	1.33	3.68
Third World (140)	5.70	2.64	3.06
OPEC (13)	9.59	4.51	5.08
Rest of Third World (127)	5.31	2.45	2.86
World	5.58	2.32	3.26

Source: *World Bank Atlas,* 1976.
[a]Excludes recently established socialist countries.

On the other hand, within the non–OPEC LDCs, several countries had outstanding growth records during 1960–1974. This was particularly true for a group of small countries in Asia—Singapore, South Korea, Taiwan, and Hong Kong—that grew at a per capita rate of 6½ percent per year and more. In addition, Puerto Rico was above 5 percent. Brazil, the Dominican Republic, and Tunisia had similar performances for the briefer period of 1965–1974.(see Table 3). Of course, some of the OPEC countries turned in even higher growth rates. In fact, on the average their growth rates easily exceeded the pace set by the advanced capitalist nations; and they greatly outdistanced the lumbering gait of the poorer Third World countries (see Tables 2 and 4). Looking ahead to 1985, the World Bank sees the continuance of fairly high growth rates for the LDCs (see Table 5).

Despite prevailing Marxist notions about dependency, neo-colonialism, the development of underdevelopment, and the

TABLE 3

MOST RAPIDLY GROWING THIRD-WORLD COUNTRIES,
NON-OPEC, 1960-1974

Country[a]	Annual Growth Rates of GNP Per Capita
Singapore	7.6
Republic of Korea	7.3
Hong Kong	6.6
Republic of China (Taiwan)	6.5
Puerto Rico	5.3
Brazil (1965-1974)	6.3
Dominican Republic (1965-1974)	5.5
Tunisia (1965-1974)	5.4

Source: *World Bank Atals*, 1976.
[a]Excluding countries with fewer than 1 million population.

like, some of the Third World countries have made considerable progress, within the capitalist mode of production, in industrializing their economies. While Marx
and Engels would probably not have been surprised by
this—"The country that is more developed industrially,"
Marx wrote, "only shows to the less developed, the
image of its own future."[4] —Paul Baran, A. G. Frank, an
and other modern-day Marxists who follow Lenin on
this more closely than Marx and Engels have something
to explain.

Baran argued that, while the imperialist nations had
had a differential and complex impact on underdeveloped countries, they had so distorted development in
much of the world that these countries could not possibly see the image of their own future in the advanced
industrial countries.[5] The principal impact of foreign
enterprise on the development of the LDCs was, Baran
alleged, "in hardening and strengthening the sway of
merchant capitalism, in slowing down and indeed

TABLE 4

PRESENT CHARACTERISTICS AND GROWTH PERFORMANCES OF THE OPEC COUNTRIES, 1974 AND 1960–1974

Countries	GNP (in 1974 US $ billions)	Population (in millions)	GNP Per Capita (in 1974 US $)	Growth Rate GNP per Capita (in 1974 US $)	Land Area (thousands of sq. miles)
Algeria	11.1	15.2	730	1.3	920
Ecuador	3.3	7.0	480	2.4	110
Gabon	1.0	.5	1,960	4.7	103
Indonesia	21.8	128.4	170	2.4	735
Iran	41.4	33.1	1,250	6.7	636
Iraq	12.0	10.8	1,110	4.0	173
Kuwait	9.3	.9	10,030	-2.7	6
Libya	10.4	2.4	4,440	12.5	680
Nigeria	20.8	73.0	280	2.9	357
Qatar	1.4	.2	7,240	5.5	8
Saudi Arabia	22.7	8.0	2,830	8.4	870
United Arab Emirates	6.1	.5	11,060	15.6	114
Venezuela	22.8	11.6	1,960	2.4	352
Total or Average	184.1	291.6	631 (weighted) 3,349 (unweighted)	5.16	5,065

Source: *World Bank Atlas*, 1976.

TABLE 5

GROWTH PROSPECTS FOR SELECTED LDCs,
1978-1985

Country Grouping	Prospective Annual Growth Rate of GDP, 1978-1985
Low-Income Countries[a]	4.3
Lower-Middle-Income Countries[b]	6.4
Intermediate-Middle-Income Countries[c]	7.2
Upper-Middle-Income Countries[d]	5.8
Capital-Deficit Oil-Exporting Countries[e]	7.0

Source: World Bank, *Prospects for Developing Countries, 1978-1985,*
November 1977.

[a]Ethiopia, Kenya, Madagascar, Tanzania, Bangladesh, India, Pakistan,
Sri Lanka.

[b]Cameroon, Ghana, Ivory Coast, Liberia, Senegal, Sudan, Phillippines,
Thailand, Bolivia, Egypt, Morocco.

[c]Zambia, Korea, Malaysia, Brazil, Chile, Colombia, Guatemala, Mexico,
Peru, Syria, Tunisia, Turkey.

[d]Argentina, Jamaica, Yugoslavia.

[e]Indonesia, Nigeria, Ecuador, Algeria, Venezuela, Iran.

preventing its transformation into industrial capitalism."[6]
He argued that economic development in these countries
boded "nothing but evil to Western capital."[7] Foreign
capital, therefore, dominated the LDCs' capitalist classes,
who, afraid of social revolutions, had struck alliances with
backward, feudal interests against the people. It was this
combination that prevented industrialization and the abolition of widespread poverty.

While some Marxists, notably Samir Amin, have gone
beyond this level of analysis (though not in a rigorous
way) by discussing the conditions under which industrialization would take place in Third World countries,
Baran's treatment has to this day set the tone for most.
But the fact is, as Bill Warren and others have demon-

strated, that at least a few dozen Third World countries
have had, for a quarter of a century, rapid rates of growth
of manufacturing (i.e., excluding mining and utilities).
Warren, relying on one of Chenery's studies, shows manufacturing growth rates during 1951–1969 of 17 percent
for Korea, 16 percent for Taiwan, 15 percent for Jordan,
the same for Singapore and Pakistan, just a bit lower for
Panama and Zambia, and so on (see Table 6). World Bank
data show a group of 40 Third World countries in 1955
with only 10 percent of their merchandise exports in
manufactures. Today that figure is around 40 percent.
The World Bank goes on to say: "All but the least developed countries have established manufacturing sectors
employing a variety of complex modern techniques, and
producing a wide range of consumption and intermediate
goods. The more industrialized developing countries also
produce capital goods. A widening range of manufactured

TABLE 6

SOME DATA ON MANUFACTURING AND INDUSTRIAL
SECTOR IN LDCs, POSTWAR PERIOD

Country	Annual Growth Rates of Manufacturing 1951–1969
Republic of Korea	16.9
Taiwan	16.1
Jordan	15.2
Pakistan	15.0
Singapore	14.8
Panama	14.2
Zambia	13.8
Turkey	11.5
Iran	11.2

Source: Bill Warren, "Imperialism and Capitalist
Industrialization," *New Left Review*, September 1973.

TABLE 6 *(continued)*

SOME DATA ON MANUFACTURING AND INDUSTRIAL
SECTOR IN LDCs, POSTWAR PERIOD

Country	Manufacturing as a percent of GDP, 1970
Mexico	23
Republic of Korea	22
Peru	21
Brazil	20
Colombia	19
Zaire	19
Venezuela	17
Philippines	16
United States	26
United Kingdom	28

Source: M. Todaro, *Economic Development in
the Third World,* p. 23.

Countries at Per Capita GDP of:	Gross Product of Industry Sector as Percent of GDP
$ 50	7.3
100	13.5
200	19.6
400	25.5
800	31.4
2,000	38.9

Source: P. Yotopoulos and J. Nugent, *Economics of Development,* p. 288. Original source is Chenery, Elkington,
and Sims, "A Uniform Analysis of Development Patterns,"
Cambridge, July 1970, Harvard Center for International
Affairs.

products is becoming competitive internationally."[8] Another study by Chenery and associates reveals that gross
product of the industrial sector as a percentage of GDP

rises steadily across a group of LDCs as their incomes per capita rise.

Although we are still in the era of (economic) neocolonialism and although Warren may be the Eduard Bernstein of this modern era, it is nevertheless true that the growth and spread of Marxism around the world and the increasing rivalry among more-evenly matched capitalist powers have enabled many LDCs to gain a measure of independence from their present and former oppressors and thus to extend and deepen their own industrialization efforts.[9] In short, circumstances have permitted many Third World countries to stand on their own feet and to pursue, in the name of nationalism, a more self-directed course toward industrialization and higher living standards.

Still, the fact is that most of the LDCs even today have manufacturing sectors that are very small compared to those in the advanced countries. They are even smaller when compared to the LDCs' own agricultural sectors, especially when the comparison is made in terms of the labor force employed in the two sectors.[10] Moreover, it has been argued by Amin and others that in many cases the advanced capitalist countries are shaping and controlling—partly through their own multinational corporations—the industrialization now going on in the LDCs. Since there is no way to stop it, the next best move is to direct and restrain it. And that, many Marxists contend, is exactly what is being done.

III. Maldistribution, Poverty, and Unemployment: The Flies in the Ointment

There is no question that recent experience with economic development has shaken the faith of many conventional economists in their own theories of growth. Gerald Meier has noted the dissatisfaction felt by many economists over some of the results of development during the 1950s and 1960s. Such discontent, bordering on bewilderment, has even reached the doors of the World Bank, as Meier explains:

> The World Bank now emphasizes that the failure to achieve a minimum level of income above the "poverty line" has kept some 40 per cent of the peoples in the less developed countries in the condition of "absolute poverty"—a condition of life so degraded by disease, illiteracy, malnutrition, and squalor as to deny its victims basic human necessities. The persistence of absolute poverty, despite respectable achievements in rates of growth in GNP, is now of more concern than that of relative poverty, or of a "widening gap" between the rich and poor countries.[11]

In 1976 the World Bank estimated, as Meier related, that, in LDCs with a total population of 1,907 million, 723 million people were living in absolute poverty—almost 40 percent of the total. This report then went on to say that the sheer weight of this poverty, despite 25 years of rapid development, is leading to a reassessment of development policies.[12] In another World Bank publication, Hollis Chenery commenced his survey of the situation by confessing: "It is now clear that more than a decade of rapid growth in underdeveloped countries has been of little or no benefit to perhaps a third of their population."[13]

Addressing himself to the same problem, but in a somewhat more Marxist way, Hans Singer wrote a few years ago: "It is now clear that rapid growth of output can, and does, go hand in hand with increased impoverishment of large sections of the population, a rapid rise in the number of people living below any acceptable poverty line, [a] rise in underemployment, and a general failure in the development process to involve larger numbers of the population."[14] Reacting similarly, Nugent and Yotopoulos recently wrote "The real surprise of the recent experience . . . is that un-

employment and inequality have been growing at historically unprecedented rates."[15]

This situation has become so scandalous, in fact, that
conventional economists in this field now seem agreed
that absolute poverty, grossly unequal incomes, and mass
unemployment constitute *the* development problem of
the times.

The data available to us from all levels of the global
capitalist structure explain why this is so. If, for example,
we combine the countries of the First and Third worlds
and rank these countries by their GNP per capita, it is all
too obvious that the wealthiest capitalist nations have the
highest growth rates while the poorest nations are barely
advancing. Thus, quite unlike the socialist countries, inequality *among* capitalist countries is becoming even larger
as time goes on. This growing disparity can be seen in
Table 7, where the countries are ranked in four groups of
20 and a final one of 29, in the manner described above.
The growth rate of GNP per capita, during 1960–1974,
declined steadily down this array. It was 4.6 percent for
the wealthiest groups, 4.3 percent for the next, and then
3.3 percent, 2.2 percent, and finally 1.0 percent for the
poorest group of countries. The growth rate of GNP itself
also declined, but not continuously and not rapidly—not
rapidly because the growth rate of population rose the
least among the wealthy and the most among the poor.
The large population gains in the poorer countries are
themselves related to insecurity, which is in turn associated
with poverty and inequalities.

There is also a discouraging amount of maldistribution
of income *within* the capitalist countries, especially in the
LDCs. Generally speaking, in the LDCs, the top 20 percent of income receivers obtain well over half of the national income, while the bottom 20 percent get only 5
percent of it. Thus the top group receives ten to eleven
times what the bottom group manages to scrape together.
Moreover, the top 20 percent receive over 4 times the

TABLE 7

ANNUAL GROWTH RATES OF ADVANCED CAPITALIST AND
NON-MARXIAN LDCs, 1960–1974, RANKED BY GNP PER CAPITA

Advanced Capitalist & Non-Marxian Countries	GNP Per Capita (1974 US $)	Population Mid-1974 (millions)	Annual Growth Rates (Unweighted), 1960–74		
			GNP Per Capita	Population	GNP
Top 20	7,870–2,820	659	4.63	1.27	5.90
Second 20	2,490–840	346	4.28	2.06	6.34
Third 20	830–470	217	3.29	2.67	5.96
Fourth 20	460–210	292	2.19	2.69	4.88
Bottom 29	200–70	1,090	0.98	2.41	3.39
5 Advanced Capitalist Countries[a]	6,670–3,590	493	4.42	0.90	5.32
25 Most Populous LDCs[b]	1,090–100	1,472	2.94	2.71	5.65

Source: *World Bank Atlas, 1976.*
[a]United States, West Germany, Japan, France, United Kingdom.
[b]India, Indonesia, Mexico, Brazil, Pakistan, Philippines, Nigeria, Bangladesh, Thailand, Republic of Korea, Algeria, Zaire, Colombia, Iran, Ethiopia, Morocco, Taiwan, Sudan, Peru, Sri Lanka, Kenya, Malaysia, Venezuela, Uganda, and Chile.

income of the bottom *40 percent* of the population (see Table 8). These data support the contention, referred to above, that a third to a half of the population in the LDCs live in what can only be described as abject or absolute poverty (see Table 9).

There is, however, some contrary evidence about income distribution. Over certain periods since 1945, income distribution seems to have improved in Taiwan, Sri Lanka, Colombia, and a few other places.[16] Further, some studies have revealed a positive, though weak, relation between rates of growth and the share of income going to the

TABLE 8

A MEASURE OF INCOME INEQUALITY
IN SELECTED THRID–WORLD COUNTRIES

Countries	*Ratio of Share of Top 20% of Income Receivers to Share of Bottom 20%*
Libya	larger than 100
Gabon	36
Iraq	34
Colombia	31
South Africa	30
Jamaica	28
Senegal	21
Lebanon	20
Brazil	18
India	5
Burma	5
Surinam	4
Niger	4
Chad	4
Median	11

Source: I. Adelman and C. T. Morris, *An Anatomy of Income Distribution in Developing Nations: A Summary of Findings,* IBRD–IDA Working Paper, September 23, 1971.

TABLE 9

ESTIMATES OF POPULATION
BELOW POVERTY LINE IN 1969
(percentages)

Region	Percentage below Poverty Line	
	US $50	US $75
Latin America	10.8	17.4
Asia	36.7	57.2
Africa	28.4	43.6
Total[a]	30.9	48.2

Source: M. S. Ahluwalia, "Income Inequality: Some Dimensions of the Problem," *Finance and Development*, September, 1974.
[a]Data are for 44 non-Marxian developing countries.

bottom 40 percent of the population.[17] Also it has been demonstrated that the developed countries generally have more equal income distributions than the LDCs, so that continued economic development by the LDCs might eventually lead them to greater equity—after, that is, they pass through a sort of purgatory phase in which income distribution seems for a time to worsen.[18]

This last point is made in Table 10, which shows very poor countries starting the growth process with rudimentary equality, proceeding into greater inequality during the initial stages of growth, but then, once this phase has been left behind, enjoying increasing equality as growth continues into higher per capita income levels. As Hagen notes, however, if the lowest-income countries are to repeat the history of the higher-income ones, "It would take more than a century and one half for countries with per capita incomes of $75 to reach an income level of $1,000 [at a two percent growth rate]," at

TABLE 10

PER CAPITA INCOME LEVELS
AND DEGREE OF INEQUALITY,
62 COUNTRIES, NON–MARXIST

Per Capita Income Level (pre-tax)	Number of Countries	Ratio of Income Share of Highest 20% to Income Share of Lowest 40%	
$100 or less	8	2.8	rudimentary equality
100–200	5	4.3	
201–300	13	6.1	higher-Gini purgatory phase
301–500	8	5.0	
501–1000	12	4.0	increasing equality
Above 1000	15	3.1	
	61	4.16	(weighted average)

Source: E. E. Hagen, *The Economics of Development,* p. 226. Original data from Chenery, et al., *Redistribution with Growth.*

which point income distribution would be substantially better than it is in the lower income ranges.[19] It is unlikely that the poor would wait that long for more equitable treatment! Furthermore, the more equal distributions in the advanced countries are owing in large part to huge and continuing government programs to offset the natural tendencies of the capitalist accumulation process to polarize incomes. Once the working classes gain sufficient strength against capital to obtain such programs, the worst inherent tendencies of capitalism can apparently be held at bay.

Another serious problem in the Third World countries is the lack of employment opportunities for increasing numbers of people. Unemployment and underemployment rates, though notoriously unreliable, are apparently high and rising in the urban areas of many LDCs. The absolute numbers of urban unemployed are expected to soar over the next several years. It is no wonder that the Marxian concept of the reserve army of labor, or its equivalent, has come to life in conventional analyses of the sources and causes of this rising unemployment in the LDCs.

What we find, therefore, is a spotty growth record within the Third World capitalist countries, some of them doing well but many foundering and, at best, a lackluster performance in the areas of equity and employment opportunities. We do not find, however, despite such a suggestion from some Marxist analyses, a uniform lack of progress among the LDCs toward industrialization, higher living standards, fairer treatment of peasants and the urban poor, or containment of the population upsurge. In these and other directions, progress has been recorded here and there within this group of countries, even though the general situation is not good.

IV. An Evaluation of Third World Development: Lessons to Be Learned

Where, then, do these considerations leave us with respect to Marxian views about economic development in the Third World?

Dialectical Development: Wealth and Poverty

I would say that recent experience has supported the Marxist contention that the development process is a dialectical one. This means that development produces not only equilibrium but its opposite, disequilibrium, not only continuities but discontinuities, both social harmonies and social conflicts, balances and imbalances, growth and stagnation, and so on. In this view of economic development, growth contains within it antigrowth forces, which will lead to the inevitable breaking up of the existing state of things, to the transiency of all things.[20] So the development process cannot be a gradual, steady, harmonious movement toward equilibrium, as seen by many advocates of neoclassical doctrine. It cannot be an uninterrupted growth process in which growth is protected from contamination against external antagonists. For the antagonists are found within the growth process itself.

A particular version of this general Marxist view is the notion that the capitalist accumulation process produces both wealth and poverty. Marx originally formulated this proposition, in the first volume of *Capital*, as the general law of capitalist accumulation. In that work, Marx wrote:

> The same causes [that] develop the expansive power of capital, develop also the labor-power at its disposal. The relative mass of the industrial reserve army increases therefore with the potential energy of wealth. . . . *This is the absolute general law of capitalist accumulation.* Like all other laws it is modified in its working by many circumstances. . . . This law rivets the laborer to capital more firmly than the wedges of Vulcan did Prometheus to the rock. It establishes an accumulation of misery, corresponding with accumulation of capital. Accumulation of wealth at one pole is, therefore, at the same time accumulation of misery, agony of toil, slavery, ignorance, brutality, mental degradation, at the opposite pole, *i.e.*, on the side of the class that produces its own product in the form of capital.[21]

In this passage, Marx had in mind not only *material* poverty (absolute and relative) at the one pole but the poverty of alienation as well, for he added that "in proportion as capital accumulates, the lot of the laborer, *be his payment high or low*, must grow worse."[22]

This thesis has been accepted by generations of Marxists, though it has often been modified in one way or another, and it has been applied in numerous ways, including applications to problems associated with underdeveloped countries. Marx and Engels paved the way for later analyses by arguing, in a dialectical manner, that European colonial expansion was an inevitable outgrowth of the development of capitalism, that it brutalized and plundered the peoples of the colonized areas and disrupted or destroyed their livelihoods, but that, despite all of this, such expansion was necessary to push many of the backward countries off dead-center so as to implant in them the seeds of capitalist development. Enrichment at one end was inextricably linked to impoverishment at the other. But the impoverishment and the brutality that accompanied it were part of a historical process in which destruction contained construction within it. The construction would be a capitalist one, Marx and Engels believed, in which the bourgeoisie would create progress and wealth at one pole, but at the same time drag masses of people "through blood and dirt, through misery and degradation." This polarization would end only with the demise of the bourgeoisie:

> When a great social revolution shall have mastered the results of the bourgeois epoch, the markets of the world and the modern powers of production, and subjected them to the common control of the most advanced peoples, then only will human progress cease to resemble that hideous pagan idol, who would not drink the nectar but from the skulls of the slain.[23]

That is just about as grisly a picture of capitalism and the wealth-poverty dichotomy it fosters as can be found anywhere.

In recent years, Paul Baran has argued that the British, while enriching themselves, "systematically destroyed all the fibres and foundations of Indian society."[24] He supported Nehru's statement that British rule and policy were responsible for the later "tragic poverty of the people."[25] Baran then set out to show how such exploitative relationships characterize the entire structure of world capitalism. In much the same way, Paul Sweezy asserted that "capitalist development inevitably produces development at one pole and underdevelopment at the other"; a proposition, he emphasized, that "applies not only to the relations between the advanced capitalist countries" and the colonial and semicolonial countries, but also within both of these parts.[26]

This thesis was generalized and carried to its ultimate destination by A. G. Frank, who contended that capitalism had long ago entered every nook and cranny of the satellite world in such a way as to make global capitalism an integrated structure of metropoles and satellites that bound nations, regions, and urban-rural areas into dominant-dependent relationships. A systematic transfer of economic surpluses continually occurred from the base of this world structure—that is, from the millions of workers and peasants—that benefited the metropoles and harmed the satellites throughout the structure, in which a lower metropolis was in turn a satellite of a higher metropolis. Frank claimed that when such exploitative ties were temporarily loosened, such as during wars or depressions involving higher metropoles, a type of development occurred in the satellites; when the ties were later strengthened, underdevelopment was generated. He also asserted that "the greater the wealth [that was] available for exploitation [in the past], the poorer and more underdeveloped the region today; and the poorer the region was as a colony, the richer and more developed it is today."[27]

Samir Amin has most recently analyzed this polarization thesis in greater depth. All peripheral or satellite formations, Amin writes, have four main characteristics: (1) the predominance of agrarian capitalism; (2) a local, mainly merchant bourgeoisie that is dominated by foreign capital;

(3) the growth of a large bureaucracy, which substitutes for an urban bourgeoisie; and (4) incomplete proletarianization, which takes the form of masses of poor peasants, urban unemployed, and many marginal workers. These are the features of an incomplete and extraverted development of local capitalism, in which the center capital reshapes the periphery into extensions of the center, thereby preventing autocentric development in the periphery and establishing unequal exchange between center and periphery—that is, differences between the returns to labor that are larger than differences between their productivities.[28] The dominance of foreign capital in the periphery, Amin claims, means distorted development toward export activities and excessive development of the tertiary sector and light industry. It also means extreme unevenness of development, the disarticulation of the economy, a development process that is not cumulative, and a strong tendency toward periphery indebtedness to the center.[29]

It is a general consensus, then, among Marxists that capitalism produces polarization, day in and day out. The basic mechanism is that capital utilizes its economic and political dominance to exploit labor throughout the global system by employing for this purpose both plain force and market forces; and that, throughout the structure, big capital dominates small capital.

There is nothing mysterious about how "plain force" has been used, for we are all familiar these days with the extramarket means employed by the United States to keep as much of the world as possible open for profitmaking activities of its corporations and for the control of resources: CIA subversion, the training and equipping of local police and military, armed invasion, the support of subimperialist powers who do the dirty work in their own areas, assassination plots against menacing foreign leaders, and so on. The evidence in this realm is overwhelmingly in favor of Marxist views of how imperialism attempts to contain movements that threaten to undermine its privileged positions of wealth and power.

When it comes to "market forces," however, Marxist theorists appear to be only in the early stages leading to a full formulation of the variety of mechanisms in the capital-accumulation process that generate biformity. Still, there have been some outstanding achievements here. Arghiri Emmanuel has analyzed how increasing inequality between nations is rooted in an unequal exchange that tends to increase over time, so that poor nations become poorer and the rich ones richer. Samir Amin has extended the analysis into processes of biformity within the satellite or periphery countries, as I previously discussed. Also, many notable contributions have been made by economists and others pursuing dependency theory, including Theotonio Dos Santos, Celso Furtado, and F. H. Cardoso. But my impression is that we still fall far short of a full understanding of how market forces, and the values and behavior patterns that support market processes, contribute to polarization of living standards at the various levels of the global capitalist system.

A convincing explanation of this must commence with the fundamental mechanism of exploitation of labor by capital. The explanation would then include the process that makes the reserve army of labor a necessary element of the capitalist mode of production and an analysis of how the expansion of this mode dispossesses and impoverishes previously self-sufficient producers. The explanation would also include an analysis of how the capitalist mode necessarily builds on efficiency, which is often antithetical to equity; of how it builds on specialization, which increases the vulnerability of people and areas to adverse developments; and of how it transfers wealth from poor areas to wealthy ones, via the price mechanism. It would then go on to discuss the values and behavior patterns, engendered and supported by the capitalist mode, which compel individuals to seek success even at the expense of others' welfare and which encourage and reward cheating and extortion of the poor by the rich. Finally, the explanation would show how poverty, once established, feeds on itself—the poor lack capital, information, education, and so on—and how wealth, once established, also feeds on itself.

Marx once said, in discussing the repeal of the Corn Laws in England: "If the free-traders cannot understand how one nation can grow rich at the expense of another, we need not wonder, since these same gentlemen also refuse to understand how within one country one class can enrich itself at the expense of another."[30] Present-day Marxists do understand these things, but they are still several steps away from having a general theory about them.

Conventional Development: Life-Cycles and Mistakes

Conventional development economists, while recognizing poverty, inequalities, and unemployment in the Third World countries, have explanations and remedies for these ills that contain enough truth to be of interest to Marxist theorists. And yet the latter have paid little attention to these orthodox rationalizations.

The principal and most general explanation of the economic ills of the Third World is that they are associated with the particular stage of a life-cycle that the LDCs happen to be in, and so can be outgrown. Thus, as one version of this explanation has it, all countries, provided they are not eternally damned to the inferno, enter a purgatory stage before they go onward and upward to blessedness and earthly paradise. Along this development path, income distribution worsens before it gets better. Population growth gets out of hand before birth rates begin to fall into line with death rates. Countries become chronic debtors before they burst into the heaven of creditors. They go through the hell of hyperinflation before they develop their economies sufficiently to allow price stabilization. The unemployed pile up in new urban centers before full employment can be enjoyed. And countries might even suffer dictatorship before democracy wins out. Another version of the life-cycle explanation—the straight-line instead of the U-shaped model—is that things start off bad and then get better and better (see Tables 5 and 10 for examples).

These explanations are meant to suggest, of course, that, when one encounters the growing ills of the Third World, one is merely looking at some childhood diseases. With proper care of the kiddies, all will be well later on. In many cases, though, the data themselves are quite underdeveloped and just barely suggest what is so confidently asserted. Moreover, the results rest on cross-section data which are intended to apply to individual countries over time. The dangers of making this leap are so well known as to require no comment from me. Also Marxists would be correct to point out that young socialist countries appear to be immune to most, and perhaps to all, of these diseases. Yet, in each of the examples that I just cited, there is a plausible hypothesis with more or less supporting data that should enlist the attention of Marxists, who, however, are too busy ascribing all ills to capitalism in general to have time to consider the orthodox arguments.

Conventional development economists have another arrow for their bow. The ills of poverty, inequality, and unemployment that one finds in Third World countries, they say, are largely owing to the gross inefficiency with which these economies are run. Their economic managers create the maladies by espousing policies that are almost insane. For example, a host of measures underprice capital and overprice labor: high minimum wage rates, too low a rate

of interest, overvalued currency (which makes imported
machinery cheap), payroll taxes on employers for their
employees, and exemptions from custom duties for imported capital equipment. Each of these measures induces
the substitution of capital for labor, thereby exacerbating
unemployment, poverty, and income inequalities. The
same thing is accomplished when policymakers neglect agriculture, which uses labor-intensive methods, and support
heavy industry, which utilizes capital-intensive methods.
Other policies, it is said, also interfere with what would
be correct relative prices, and the resulting distortions are
enough to make anyone sick.

The World Bank has recently set forth a similar explanation of poverty and other bourgeois ills. There has been
a poor ordering, the Bank says, of national priorities. A
reordering is called for. Instead of policies to foster "growth
in general," policies should be redesigned to direct investment to poverty groups in the form of education, access
to credit, health care, public facilities, and so on. Thus,
the new national priorities should be "growth," as before,
but growth in the lower income groups where absolute
poverty resides.[31]

Just as in the previous set of arguments, the intention
here is to make one believe that the growing ills one sees
in young capitalist economies are not owing to capitalism
per se but to the appalling way the economies are managed.
If the distortions or improper national priorities were cor-
rected, the argument goes, the economic ills would be
cured. In this case, too, there is probably enough truth
behind the argument to warrant the attention of Marxists.
But even granting this, Marxists must go on to ask, as
conventional economists do not, why there is so much inefficiency and ineptness. Does it serve a political purpose?
Which class does it help, and how? Or is it simply due to
ignorance? Conventional economists believe much too
naively that no one wants unemployment or poverty, and

so they must arise from lack of knowledge or will power. Marxists know that such seeming disorders are often beneficial to ruling classes, and hence are no mistakes at all but outcomes of rational policies. While I believe that Marxists are mainly correct about this, it is still true that the inefficiencies and absurdities, willful or not, are well worth studying. Marxists themselves are too prone to assume that all capitalist economies, at whatever stage of development they find themselves, are run with equal efficiency. There is much for Marxists to learn in this area.

Conventional Development: The Population Explosion

Many conventional economists ascribe the ills of the LDCs in part to the population explosion that is taking place throughout the Third World. It is claimed that this is so unusual in history and so devastating as to account for much of the poverty and inequality that one observes everywhere.

Marxists have assumed that the so-called population problem is meant to divert attention from the real issues, which involve the transformation of the present exploitative economic systems into socialist societies. I think that Marxists are largely correct about this. Underdevelopment—with its low growth rates, high levels of unemployment, harsh income inequalities, widespread lack of education, the dominance of rural living, and the oppression of females—is closely associated with high birth rates and so with high rates of population growth.[32] Thus, if ruling classes, through their exploitation of working classes and in other ways, generate underdevelopment, the consequence is likely to be high population growth rates, which in turn feed back to lower incomes per capita and more underdevelopment. The overthrow of these ruling classes is a necessary, though not a sufficient, condition for breaking this vicious cycle.

While all of this is largely true, Marxists have not taken adequate account of the reasons for and the consequences of the population explosion that has occurred in recent decades. World population up to 1650 grew by only a small fraction of 1 percent per annum. For the next 300 years the rate crept up toward 1 percent. But in the last two or three decades it has risen to around 2 percent or more—1 percent in the developed countries and 2½ percent in the less developed ones. Between A.D. 1 and 1750, world population rose by 480 million. In the next 200 years, it rose by 1,750 million, and in the last 28 years by the same amount. China and India alone this year will add about 30 million to the world's population, a number that exceeds the *total* national population of 87 percent of the countries of the world.

The major reason for this explosion is the decline in death rates owing to rapid technological advances in modern medicine—especially vaccination against malaria, smallpox, yellow fever, and cholera—and to the spread of modern public health measures. The sharp drop in death rates generated a very high natural rate of increase because both birth and death rates in the LDCs were a percentage point higher than they had been in preindustrial Europe (4½ against 3½percent). All of this has created serious difficulties for many countries in the Third World, unlike the nineteenth-century experience of western Europe when both death and birth rates declined slowly and together.[33]

Although there is evidence that a new global demographic transformation is now underway, involving declining birth rates to match the previous drop in death rates, population pressure for many LDCs will remain intense and will retard improvements in living standards for hundreds of millions of people for many years to come. This is a problem that concerns both socialist and capitalist countries. Some countries in both camps have succeeded in recent years in getting their population problems somewhat under control—socialist China as well as capitalist Taiwan and Singapore. Thus there would appear to be some mechanisms within the capitalist mode of production that, to some degree, control population upsurges, and these ought to be more carefully investigated by Marxist development economists than they have been in the past.

The Testing of Theories

A serious failing of Marxist development economists lies in their lack of interest in testing theory against the facts. Almost without exception, it has been the conventional economists who have dug out the information on income inequalities, differential growth rates, absolute poverty, unemployment, and the like. Even with these data available, Marxists appear uninterested in them and, instead, remain totally absorbed in more model building. An unfriendly critic would say that Marxists ignore these data because they disprove their theories. A better and more profound explanation is that Marxists are trained to be highly suspicious of surface phenomena and the crude empiricism often used in analyzing these outward manifestations of deeper, underlying realities. Marx prepared the way for this attitude with his analysis of the production and circulation spheres of the accumulation process; in the former, located in the underworld, so to speak, resided the reality of exploitation, while in the latter, located on the surface of everyday life, "equality and freedom" reigned. Surface data, therefore, could badly mislead one, could create fantastic illusions about how the system really operated. Ever since that brilliant analysis of Marx, his followers have been extremely wary of all such superficial evidence.

But this attitude is wrong. Marx himself used plentiful data in his major work. These "facial expressions" of capitalism are extremely useful to the investigator, so long as he or she is aware of what is really going on underneath it all. Since there are systematic relations between the one world and the other, Marxist theories about the underlying realities can be tested against the surface data with good effect. Indeed, Marxists ought to be in a better position than conventional economists to provide analytical depth to the interpretation of these data.

In any event, Marxists ought to look carefully at what conventional economists call the "success stories" of capitalist economic development and, indeed, at all the evidence that has been so laboriously compiled by the more orthodox economists, no matter how embarrassing it may be. One would not think it necessary to say that, but it is.

V. Summary of Marxist and Orthodox Responses

A large number of non-Marxian LDCs are stagnating. Many, however, are expanding, but, even in these cases, their growth is often accompanied by growing inequities, unemployment, and impoverishment. Orthodox economists look on these "ills" either as childhood diseases or as residues of the past and, hence, either curable with time and patience or capable of being gradually mopped up. Marxists, on the other hand, believe that capitalist development itself creates these so-called ills, day in and day out, along with society's wealth. Furthermore, orthodox economists think that the "ills" are truly social maladies not desired by society, while Marxists are convinced that they often serve a useful function for the ruling classes and hence are results of rational, purposive policies. These are two entirely different ways of looking at the development process. The first suggests reform; the second revolution. Indeed, Marxists believe that the very processes of capitalist accumulation create the revolutionary conditions required for overthrowing capitalism and establishing more humane socialist societies.

In fact, for the better part of this century, capitalism *has* been overthrown in large parts of the world, and Marxism has taken over these areas. These are the countries I shall discuss next.

VI. Comparative Performances of Socialist Countries

There are now about 24 Marxist socialist countries that produce a fifth of the world's GNP and have roughly a third of the global population and land area.[34] In addition, Marxists control numerous local governments in many countries, notably in France and Italy, and Marxism as a national movement is strong not only in those two countries but also in India, Japan, Greece, Portugal, Spain, and elsewhere. Many liberation movements and guerrilla operations fight under the red banner of Marxism.

The Soviet Union and China dominate the Marxian group. They have 80 percent of the group's population and land area, and they produce almost three-quarters of its GNP. However, when it comes to income per capita, three countries beat the Soviet Union—Poland, the German Democratic Republic, and Czechoslovakia—and all but seven of them appear to be ahead of China (see Table 11).

Thirteen of the countries calling themselves Marxist existed in 1960, and since that time their GNP annual growth rates have averaged about 5 percent while their populations have grown at 1.3 percent. Thus the rate of advance of GNP per capita in these countries has been 3.7 percent, a percentage point higher than in the non–OPEC Third World (see Tables 1 and 2). Within this group of thirteen Romania, China, and Yugoslavia are at the top of the growth hit-parade, while Cuba, Mongolia, and Czechoslovakia are at the bottom.

Marxism versus Capitalism: Growth Performances

There are many ways to compare the growth performances of Marxist countries to those of other countries.
Following one method, I have chosen to list the thirteen
Marxist countries by size of population against an equal
number of the most populous non-Marxian LDCs, also
ranked by population size. Both groups have about the
same total population. For the groups as a whole, the
Marxian countries had a somewhat better growth record
than the others. Considering only parts of the two groups,
China and the Soviet Union far outperformed India and
Indonesia; the top five Marxian countries easily beat the
five most-populous LDCs; and the same is true when the
top ten in each group are matched (see Table 12).

While, as I mentioned previously, the Marxian group
had a better growth record than all of the non–OPEC
LDCs combined, there were, nevertheless, several countries in the latter group that compiled superior records to
the Marxian ones. However, these countries are, for the
most part, either tiny city-states (Singapore and Hong
Kong) or recipients of massive U.S. aid (Republic of
Korea and Republic of China). A few others, however,
such as Brazil and Thailand, can be more fairly compared
with the Marxian countries, and their growth rates are at
least as good (see Table 3). Several of the OPEC nations,
of course, had growth rates above those found in Marxist
countries.

Another test is to compare the eastern European coun-
tires, including the Soviet Union, to the nations of western
Europe. The result is a virtual tie, with each group growing, from 1960 to 1974, at about 4.3 percent per annum
(see Table 13). I have also made sib-comparisons of ten
pairs of Marxian and capitalist countries, and in most
cases the capitalist country wins. For example, Taiwan
beats mainland China, south Korea does better than the
north, Austria wins over Hungary, Greece over Albania,

TABLE 11

GNP, POPULATION, GNP PER CAPITA, AND LAND AREA IN MARXIAN SOCIALIST COUNTRIES, 1974

Countries	Population (in millions)	GNP (in 1974 US $ billions)	GNP Per Capita (in 1974 US $)	Land Area (thousands of sq. miles)
People's Republic of China	809	$ 245	$ 300	3,692
USSR	252	599	2,380	8,649
Socialist Republic of Vietnam	44	7	150	127
Poland	34	85	2,510	121
Ethiopia[b]	27	3	100	471
Yugoslavia	21	28	1,310	99
Romania	21	23	1,100	92
German Democratic Republic	17	63	3,710	42
Democratic People's Republic of Korea	15	6	390	47
Czechoslovakia	15	49	3,330	49
Hungary	10	23	2,180	36

Cuba	9	6	710	44
Mozambique	9	3	340	302
Bulgaria	9	15	1,780	43
Cambodia	8	1	70	70
Angola	6	4	710	481
People's Democratic Republic of Yemen	2	a	220	39
Lao People's Democratic Republic	3	a	70	92
Somalia[b]	3	a	90	246
People's Republic of Benin[b]	3	a	120	44
Albania	2	1	530	11
Mongolia	1	1	610	593
Guyana[b]	1	a	500	83
Guinea-Bissau	1	a	390	14
Total or Average	1,322	1,164	983[c]	15,487

Source: *World Bank Atlas*, 1976, and U.N. *Statistical Yearbook*, 1976. [a]Less than $500 million. [b]Doubtful inclusion. [c]Unweighted average.

TABLE 12

ANNUAL GROWTH RATES OF
GNP PER CAPITA DURING 1960-1974,
COUNTRIES RANKED BY SIZE OF POPULATION

Marxian Socialist		*Non-Marxian LDCs*	
People's Republic of China	5.2	India	1.1
Union of Soviet		Indonesia	2.4
Socialist Republics	3.8	Brazil	4.0
Poland	4.0	Bangladesh	-0.5
Yugoslavia	4.9	Nigeria	2.9
Romania	8.0[a]	Pakistan	3.4
German Democratic		Mexico	3.3
Republic	3.1	Philippines	2.4
Democratic People's		Thailand	4.6
Republic of Korea	4.4	Turkey	3.9
Czechoslavakia	2.4	Egypt	1.5
Hungary	3.2	Republic of Korea	7.3
Cuba	-0.9	Iran	6.7
Bulgaria	4.5		
Albania	4.4	Top 2	1.75
Mongolia	0.8	Top 5	1.98
		Top 10	2.75
Top 2	4.50	Top 2	1.75
Top 5	5.18	Top 5	1.98
Top 10	3.81	Top 10	2.75
All 13	3.68	All 13	3.31

Source: *World Bank Atlas,* 1976.   [a]1965-1974.

TABLE 13

ANNUAL GROWTH RATES OF GNP PER CAPITA
OF EASTERN AND WESTERN EUROPE,
1960-1974, UNWEIGHTED AVERAGES

Eastern Europe[a]	4.26
Western Europe[b]	4.34

Source: *World Bank Atlas*, 1976.
[a]Includes the Union of Soviet Socialist Republics.
[b]Includes Turkey, Greece, Finland, and Cyprus.

and so on. For the group, the capitalist growth rate was more than a full percentage point above that of the Marxian countries. Only if Yugoslavia is compared to Italy and Bulgaria to Turkey would Marxian countries do better than their capitalist counterparts (see Table 14).

Finally, a comparison of the growth performances of the USSR and the United States, during 1950–1975, reveals a clear-cut victory for the Marxist side. In these 25 years, the Soviets were far superior in this respect in industrial production and somewhat better in agriculture. Their growth rate of GNP was two percentage points higher than that of the United States. As a consequence, their GNP per capita rose from 28 percent of that of the United States in 1950 to 44 percent in 1975 (see Table 15). But, of course, there are several advanced capitalist countries that have growth records either equal to or superior to that of the Soviet Union.

In summary, the picture here is a mixed one: the Marxist countries have on the whole a very good growth performance, but it is not, by every comparison, superior to that of capitalist countries. Marxists can be pleased with the general result, but they cannot be satisfied with the growth achievements of a few of the socialist countries. Cuba, especially, has been somewhat of a disappointment, although there are certainly well-known mitigating circumstances associated with her development. A few of the eastern European countries have also lagged rather badly. More important, the per capita growth rate of the USSR has been on a falling trend throught the postwar period—roughly 5 percent in the 1950s, 4 percent in the 1960s, and 3 percent thus far in the 1970s. It is evident that growth is now considerably more difficult for the Soviets than it used to be. China, too, has shown some signs of stress in this regard in the last few years.[35]

Marxists have always had a strong belief that socialism can outproduce capitalism. But very few Marxists in "western" countries have bothered to look closely at

TABLE 14

SIB-COMPARISONS OF ANNUAL GROWTH RATES
OF GNP PER CAPITA, 1960–1974

Marxian Socialist		*Capitalist*	
Hungary	3.2	Austria	4.4
Democratic People's Republic of Korea	4.4	Republic of Korea	7.3
People's Republic of China	5.2	Republic of China	6.5
German Democratic Republic	3.1	Federal Republic of Germany	3.7
Albania	4.4	Greece	6.8
Bulgaria	4.5	Turkey	3.9
Cuba	-0.9	Jamaica	3.6
Cuba	-0.9	Dominican Republic	3.1
Yugoslavia	4.9	Greece	6.8
Yugoslavia	4.9	Italy	4.2
Unweighted Average (8 countries)	3.6	Unweighted Average (9 countries)	4.8

Source: *World Bank Atlas,* 1976.

the comparative records. It would be especially useful if Marxists would study the sib-comparisons I mentioned a moment ago, for they do challenge the fundamental notion of socialist superiority. Further, this notion rests largely on the belief that socialist planning always beats capitalist markets; and yet in recent years much has gone wrong with central planning, particularly in the Soviet Union. Again, most "western" Marxists appear to be too busy criticizing capitalism to have time to study this problem. Maurice Dobb was one of the exceptions. Although he argued that socialist planning is capable of achieving higher and more stable growth rates than capitalist market economies, he nevertheless analyzed recent weaknesses of Soviet planning, e.g., its greater success at "extensive"

TABLE 15

USSR AND USA: COMPARATIVE GROWTH RATES,
1950–1975

	USSR	USA
Real GNP	5.2	3.3
Industrial production	7.6	3.9
Agricultural production	2.5	1.9
Population	1.4	1.4
Iron and steel	7.0	2.5–3.0
Real consumption	4.9–5.4	3.3
Real fixed investment	8.1	2.4
Real per capita disposable income	5.3–6.8	2.5

Year	GNP per capita Soviet–US Ratio
1928	.21
1940	.28
1950	.28
1960	.37
1970	.42
1975	.44

Source: *Economic Report of the President*, January 1977. Joint Economic Committee, *Soviet Economic Prospects for the Seventies*, p. 393. JEC, *Soviet Economy in a New Perspective*, pp. 246, 275, 631, 646, and 653.

than at "intensive" development and the problems encountered with faulty planning targets and poor success indicators. He and others have pointed to the poor quality of goods produced, the inappropriate price structures, the increasing difficulties of designing consistent plans, the system's discouragement of innovation, the expanding bureaucracies, and the ever-present shortages of this and surpluses of that.[36] Central planning also has its strong points; it has proved this many times in Soviet and Chinese development over the years. But a critical appraisal of this experience by Marxists is now called for.

Marxism versus Capitalism: Other Considerations

The socialist countries have not only grown rapidly, on the average, but they have had an excellent record of distributing the fruits of their growth in highly equitable ways. Income distribution is apparently much more equal in the socialist countries than in the non-Marxist LDCs or in the advanced capitalist countries. The bottom 40 percent of families receive about 25 percent of national income in socialist countries, roughly 16 percent in the advanced capitalist countries, and around an average of 12 percent in the LDCs (see Table 16). Since property income is fairly large and highly concentrated in most capitalist countries, the elimination of this factor alone in socialist countries accounts for much of the differences in the above data. Additional figures show that the top 20 percent of income receivers in five socialist countries had only 1.5 times the income of the bottom 40 percent. This ratio, in ten of the thirteen most-populous LDCs previously considered, was a very high 4.2. Mexico, Turkey, and Brazil are the worst offenders in this regard (see Table 17). Many of the smaller LDCs, which are excluded from this list, also had very high ratios of inequality. These include Rhodesia, Iraq, and many Latin American countries where the top 20 percent get as much as 10 times the share of the bottom 40 percent.[37] Moreover, there is much evidence that income is distributed fairly in a number of socialist countries, such as China, Korea, and Cuba, which are not in the tabulation.

The OECD in Paris recently compared the income received by the top and bottom 10 percent of families in eleven advanced capitalist countries. The ratio of the top to the bottom share ranged from 22 for France to 15 for the United States and seven for Sweden and the Netherlands. Roughly similar data for the Soviet Union show a ratio of 14 in 1946 dropping to under 5 in 1966. Thus, at the present time, it is probably true that the Soviet

TABLE 16

SOME DATA ON INCOME INEQUALITY
IN THE "THREE WORLDS"

Country Grouping	Share of Income of Bottom 40% of Income Receivers	Ratio of Share of Top 20% to Share of Bottom 40% of Income Receivers
Non-Marxian LDCs	12	4.5
Advanced Capitalist	16	3.0
Marxian Socialist	25	1.5

Source: M. S. Ahluwalia, "Income Inequality: Some Dimensions of the Problem," in Chenery, et al., *Redistribution with Growth*, pp. 7–9.

TABLE 17

INCOME SHARE OF TOP 20 PERCENT AS RATIO
OF INCOME SHARE OF BOTTOM 40 PERCENT
OF INCOME RECEIVERS
(VARIOUS DATES)

Marxian Socialist		Non-Marxian LDCs[a]	
Poland (1969)	1.54	India (1964)	3.25
Yugoslavia (1968)	2.24	Brazil (1970)	6.15
Czechoslovakia (1964)	1.12	Nigeria	over 4.00
Hungary (1969)	1.40	Pakistan (1964)	1.71
Bulgaria (1962)	1.24	Mexico (1969)	6.10
		Philippines (1965)	4.64
Unweighted Average	1.51	Thailand (1970)	2.68
		Turkey (1968)	6.54
		Republic of Korea (1970)	2.50
		Iran (1968)	4.36
		Unweighted Average	4.19

Source: P. A. Yotopoulos and J. Nugent, *Economics of Development*, pp. 240–41 and M. Todaro, *Economic Development in the Third World*, pp. 105–6. The original sources are M. S. Ahluwalia, "Income Inequality: Some Dimensions of the Problem," in H. B. Chenery, et al., *Redistribution with Growth*, 1974; and Irma Adelman and Cynthia Taft Morris, *Society, Politics and Economic Development: A Quantitative Approach*.

[a]The ten most populous non-Marxian LDCs for which data were available.

Union has an income distribution that is more equal than that found in any of the advanced capitalist countries (see Table 18).

The Soviets' success in narrowing income disparities since Stalin's death is attested to by many outside, usually nonsympathetic, observers. For instance, Bronson and Severin stated, in a report to the Joint Economic Committee of the U.S. Congress: "The narrowing of wage differentials in the USSR over the past two decades has been enormous."[38] Peter Wiles commented: "Since Stalin's death, I doubt that any country can show a more rapid and sweeping progress toward equality [that the Soviet Union]."[39]

TABLE 18

INCOME DISTRIBUTION IN USSR
AND ADVANCED CAPITALIST COUNTRIES

		Ratio of Share of Top 10% of Income Receivers to Share of Bottom 10%
USSR[a]	1946	14.0
	1966	4.5
France[b]		21.8
Spain		19.0
Australia		15.8
Canada		15.4
United States		15.4
West Germany		10.9
Japan		10.3
Great Britain		10.0
Norway		9.1
Sweden		7.2
Netherlands		6.8

Source: Paul R. Gregory and Robert C. Stuart, *Soviet Economic Structure and Performance,* p. 399; and *New York Times,* September 10, 1976.
[a]Excludes collective farm families.
[b]After-tax income for the countries listed, in the early 1970s.

One author even titled his article on this topic "The Soviet Income Revolution."[40]

This income revolution was achieved through a series
of measures, extending over 15 years, that raised wages
of the lowest income groups, especially in the services
sector, raised the minimum-wage rate of urban workers
by more than a third and of rural workers by about a
half, raised by more than a third the minimum pensions
of disabled workers and the minimum benefits of survi-
vors, established a national social insurance system for
peasants, similar to the one for workers, lowered taxes
on low-income families, promoted greater geographical
equality through state investments, and in general considerably narrowed the gap between urban and rural living standards. In the last 25 years, real disposable income
per capita in the Soviet Union has grown by about 6 percent per year, which is well over twice the rate in the
United States, and many of these gains have gone to the
lower income groups. This has been, indeed, an income
revolution.

Although comparable data do not exist for China,
scholars generally agree that living standards in that country, while still low, are about as uniform among the population as can be found anywhere in the world. This was
achieved by eliminating private property incomes—through
land reforms, rural collectivization, and industrial nation-
alization. In addition, industrial real wages were held back
—there was only a 7 percent rise for the entire period of
1957–1975—and this aided in narrowing the gap in rural-
urban living standards. In the meantime, the state reduced
the agricultural tax in several steps and, through changes
in relative prices, improved agriculture's terms of trade
with the urban areas. Since the mid-1950s, agriculture's
sale prices have doubled while the prices of industrial
goods sold in rural areas have remained fairly stable.
Further, living standards have become more equal through

the equitable rationing of essential goods; and social services, such as education, medical care, and housing, have been evenly distributed among the population. The state has also taken measures to increase regional equality through its centralized planning apparatus. Enterprise profits go into the state budget and much state investment from this budget has been allocated to the poorer regions. Skilled labor and technical and managerial manpower have also been allocated to poorer areas. Since the cultural revolution, 12 million young people have been sent from cities to rural areas. Finally, these measures leading to greater equality have been protected by overall price stability throughout the economy.[41]

Consequently, all the evidence that we have indicates the definite superiority of socialism over capitalism along this important dimension of economic development.

While hard numbers are not available, there are strong reasons for believing that the socialist countries as a group have substantially lower rates of abject poverty and unemployment than the mass of LDCs. Unemployment, poverty, and inequity are very serious problems in many of the LDCs, and in fact they constitute *the* current development problem in those countries. The socialist countries, while not free of these diseases, have made much more progress in finding cures for them. Similarly, socialism has a generally superior record in reducing illiteracy, cultural and educational deprivation, poor health, other nagging hazards of life, and the mental and physical suffering that so many of the world's poor are burdened with. Thus, in all of these respects, socialism has more than met the test.

While socialism's accomplishments in these areas are good, there have been some worrisome revelations. To begin with, there are indications in some of these countries of growing bureaucracies and elitist strata, the members of which have gained incomes and economic and social privileges, e.g., access to superior education, better health

care, foreign travel, and luxury imports, far above levels
contemplated by the traditions of Marxism. Further, in
some socialist countries wage differentials and urban-rural
disparities continue to be large and to show few signs of
narrowing. Work incentives remain predominantly individu-
alistic and materialistic in parts of the socialist camp, and
work relations are not progressing rapidly from hierarchical,
capitalist forms to worker-democratic ones. In short, some
socialist countries would seem to be making little if any progress toward the classless society that Marx and Lenin visualized as the communist stage beyond that of socialism.

VII. China's Economic Development

It is understandable, I suppose, that many people around
the world, including Marxist economists, have turned to
China in recent years for guidance on socialist economic
development. This is not only because the Soviet Union
has disappointed many of her former supporters but also
because, in most respects, China's development efforts have
been successful and therefore appealing. On the other hand,
these efforts have been denounced and even ridiculed by
the Soviets, who in turn have been the target of the Chinese. These are now my topics.

China's Achievements

Even if one looks at China through the narrow eyes of
conventional, growth-fixated economists, there is much to
applaud. Although progress has by no means been steady,
China's income per capita is now about 2.5 times its level
of 1952. Most of this gain has been in industrial production, which is presently 12 times its 1952 level, and lesser
amounts have been in agricultural production, which has
recently reached about 1.8 times its earlier level. Within

industrial production, substantial gains have been made in
the production of crude oil, machinery of all kinds, chem-
ical fertilizer, electric power, and cement. While iron and
steel output has risen by over 12 percent a year since
1952, in the past decade the Chinese have had problems
in this area. Highways, railroad tracks, and communication
networks have been greatly extended throughout the country. Within agriculture, grain output has kept ahead of
population, but not by much. There have been notable
gains, however in the production of fruits and vegetables,
fish products, and some meats. There is no reason these
days for anyone in China to be physically weakened by a
shortage of food. China has accomplished these results
mostly through her own efforts, though substantial help
was received in the 1950s from the USSR and other Marxist countries, and China's foreign trade has been a constant
though rather small, factor in explaining these gains. (Much
of the above information is in Table 19.)

If one looks beyond these statistics to other economic
and social terrain, however, one encounters those particular successes that have especially appealed to others in the
Third World: the spread of good health care throughout
the vast rural areas; the dramatic reduction of illiteracy
and the availability of basic education to most children;
the equitable distribution of essential consumption items
throughout the population; the organization of people for
the accomplishment of gigantic tasks, such as reforestation,
dam construction, and improvements in public sanitation;
the dissemination of cultural activities to even the remotest
parts of the country; and the call for service to others, for
selflessness, frugality, modesty, and the other qualities that
so often attract people of religion, seemingly with embar-
rassment, to this atheistic, Marxist land.

The Maoist Strategy

These characteristics that distinguish Chinese economic
development are mostly the imprints of Mao Tse-tung. The

development problem formulated by Mao was how to
build up the country's productive forces (i.e., its material
and human means of production) in ways that also in-
sured progress toward communism (i.e., toward a highly
productive and classless society). It was Mao's belief that,
if the growth of productive forces were pursued to the
neglect of the communist goal—if technical transformation
drove out social transformation—then existing social institutions and ideology would revert to, or solidify into,
capitalist forms. This, as Mao saw it, would in time damage
the development of the productive forces and the welfare
of the masses. On the other hand, the one-sided pursuit
of communist values and institutions would leave such social transformation hanging in the air, without the technical or the human means of sustaining and supporting it.
The two goals could be sought, Mao believed, in a mutually
reinforcing way. It was not necessary, in his view, to have
to sacrifice some of one goal for more of the other.

Mao's solution to this problem was to involve actively
the masses of people in the decisions and tasks of changing their world, that is, in the class struggles and technical and social transformations of their country. If people
change their world, instead of having it done for them,
they gather information about the world and so change
their own perceptions of it. At the same time, they enhance their ability and desire to change the world further.
Only through such a dialectical process, Mao thought, is
it possible for people to shake off their passivity, blind
obedience to authority, fatalistic attitudes, lack of awareness of the real world around them, fear of organization,
and their propensity for mystical and supernatural explanations of physical and social phenomena. Only through
such mass movements are people able to create new socialist institutions, weaken the continually emerging bourgeois
tendencies, develop new values to live and work by, and
dramatically raise their overall productivity in such a way
that each of these elements reinforces the others. Thus,

TABLE 19

SOME OUTPUT DATA OF THE PEOPLE'S REPUBLIC OF CHINA, SELECTED YEARS 1952-1977

(in million metric tons unless otherwise specified)

	GNP (1976 US $ billions)	Mid-Year Population (in millions)	Grain[a]	Cotton	Crude Steel	Crude Oil
1952	87	570	161	1.3	1.3	0.4
1957	122	640	191	1.6	5.4	1.5
1959	138	669	171	1.2	13.4	3.7
1965	165	750	194	1.9	12.5	11.0
1969	199	821	215	1.8	16.0	20.4
1976	324	927	285	2.3	23.0	83.6
1977	—	940	287	—	25.5	90.0
Annual Growth Rate						
1952-77	5.6%[c]	2.0%	2.3%	2.4%[c]	12.6%	24.2%
1969-77	7.2%[e]	1.7%	3.7%	3.6%[e]	6.0%	20.4%

	Chemical Fertilizer	Cement	Coal	Electric Power (bil kwh)	Industrial Production Index 1957=100	Agricultural Production Index 1957=100
1952	0.2	2.9	66	7.3	48	83
1957	0.8	6.9	131	19.3	100	100
1959	1.9	12.3	300	42.0	173	84
1965	7.6	16.3	220	42.0	199	104
1969	11.3	22.5	258	60.0	266	113
1976	27.9[b]	49.3	448	121.0[b]	502	148
1977	—	—	490	—	570	—
Annual Growth Rate						
1952–77	23.6%[c]	12.5%[c]	8.3%	13.0%[d]	10.4%	2.4%
1969–77	17.1%	11.9%[e]	8.3%	12.4%[f]	10.0%	3.9%

Source: C.I.A., *China: Economic Indicators*, October, 1977; *Far Eastern Economic Review*, January 6, 1978; Judith Banister, "China's Demographic Transition in the Asian Context," a part of her Ph.D. dissertation, presented at the Conference on the Modern Chinese Economy in a Comparative Context, Stanford University, January 8, 1977.

Note: The GNP growth rates differ in this table from those in Tables 12 and 14.

[a] Includes soybeans and converts potatoes to a grain equivalent by taking one-fifth of their actual weight.   [b]1975   [c]1952–76   [d]1952–75   [e]1969–76   [f]1969–75

for Mao, it was practical, revolutionary activity that solved the problem of socialist development—a development, I want to emphasize, that, in Mao's eyes, included giant gains in production, a goal that he always pursued.

Mao's general solution to the development problem encompassed the conviction that it was not necessary to develop fully the new productive forces before social transformation took place. In fact, Mao asserted, it was often necessary to revolutionize the relations of production first in order to release the productive forces. "Our revolution," he wrote, "began with Marxist-Leninist propaganda, which served to create new public opinion in favor of the revolution. Moreover, it was possible to destroy the old production relations only after we had overthrown a backward superstructure in the course of revolution. After the old production relations had been destroyed new ones were created, and these cleared the way for the development of new social productive forces. With that behind us we were able to set in motion the technological revolution to develop social productive forces on a large scale. At the same time, we still had to continue transforming the production relations and ideology."[42] Mao thought that this was a universal law of development.

In keeping with this prescription, Mao advocated rapid collectivization of agriculture in the mid-1950s while other, more traditional Marxists were urging the expansion of agricultural productive forces before determined efforts were made to collectivizie. Mao's position rested on his belief that, if collectivization were pushed first, it would help to expand and improve the productive forces then and there, because these forces included the peasants, whose productivity would rise by way of a learning process, as they engaged in such mass movements. Furthermore, these movements of social transformation would organize the poor and so consolidate their political power in the countryside. Collectivization would also aid in equalizing incomes and insuring that the fruits of future progress would be shared equitably. This would raise the enthusiasm of the masses for socialist institutions and so guarantee that their higher potential productivity would in fact be brought into play. Mao also thought that such drives would bring to the fore "many fine people," who would become leaders and exemplars. Finally, collectivization was immediately necessary to increase agricultural output, to prepare the way for the efficient use of modern machinery on a large scale, and to quicken the pace of light industry so that more accumulation funds could be obtained and applied to heavy industry.[43]

If one followed the "theory of productive forces," on the other hand, polarization (of wealth and poverty) would occur in the countryside. "If socialism does not occupy the rural position," Mao said, "capitalism inevitably will. . . ."[44] This would result in lower overall productivity, less enthusiasm for hard work, and anarchic diversity of efforts and goals. In the end, little progress would be made toward building highly productive material and human resources, and retrogression would occur in the goal of attaining communism.

The Present Situation

Mao's views on development are still a bone of contention within the Chinese Communish party.[45] The present leadership of the CCP has accused the "Gang of Four" of a one-sided approach to this problem: too much emphasis on "revolution" and too little on "production," too much on struggle and too little on unity. While these charges seem to have some basis, the economic fact should not be lost in the welter of accusations that China's real GNP, from the end of the cultural revolution in early 1969 through 1975, grew between 8 and 9 percent per year, which is

only a little short of spectacular, and it is even superior
to the record of the first five-year plan. If the "Gang of
Four," who rose to prominence during the cultural revolution, set out to sabotage production in the ensuing years
by creating dissension at all levels of government and by
other means, they were certainly inept! It could better be
argued that the "Gang of Four" were more successful in
1976, when production did stagnate, but, if so, they had
abundant aid from the gods on high who not only took
away Chou and Mao but caused the earth to split under
Tangshan. I conclude that, while the "Gang of Four"
probably were one-sided in their approach to the development problem, they had little impact during these years
on the economic performance of the country. If, however,
they had gained real power after Mao's death, their one-
sided policies might well have damaged the country's production capabilities. But these conclusions, I am compelled
to note, are drawn without benefit of response from the
accused.

I am on more certain ground in noting that the present
leaders have placed their emphasis on production and not
revolution, on unity and not struggle, and on responsibility
and authority in enterprises and not on mass participation.
Their stress is on making "China a great, powerful and
modern socialist country before the end of this century."
But they have failed to analyze how to accomplish this
while at the same time making progress toward communism.
Instead, the leaders stress the considerable length of the
historical period of socialism, as though to say that there
is no sense at this early stage in seriously planning for
communism. This one-sided emphasis on production, unity,
and authority is bound to disturb those who find validity
in the Maoist approach. It is possible, however, that all of
this is nothing more than an attempt to bring balance to
a situation that threatened to become increasingly one-
sided the other way.

It should be noted, too, that Mao never advocated or followed a straight-line path. For Mao, progress was a wavelike motion—a process of "cutting loose," then resting, then "cutting loose" again. Thus, to judge the present leaders fairly, in regard to their adherence to Maoist policies and goals, a longer period of observation is required than we have had. After the disasters of 1976, this is undoubtedly the time for consolidation, unity, stability, and rest from mass revolutionary movements. While Mao might agree, he would also point out that contradictions are universal, that progress is made by discovering the correct methods, i.e., the forms of struggle, for resolving them, and that unity contains disunity as its opposite in struggle. Chairman Hua Kuo-feng took note of some of this in his report to the Eleventh Party Congress, when he said: "Stability and unity do not mean writing off class struggle." Only with time will these words take on their true meaning.

In any case, the present leaders are not entirely free to chart their own course. They will find that, if their actions are to be effective, they will have to conform to circumstances "directly found, given and transmitted from the past." People make their own history, as Marx said in the *Eighteenth Brumaire,* but not exactly as they please. The important issue, then, becomes the extent to which these circumstances transmitted from the past include widely-held Maoist aims, values, practices, institutions, and so on; whether, in other words, the Maoist solutions for economic and social progress are by this time embedded in Chinese society, right down to the village level. If they are, the present leaders, or their successors, will be drawn to them; if they are not, the past will still circumscribe the future actions of the leaders, but in other ways. In any event, these new leaders do not have a clean slate on which to trace out any path that strikes their fancy.

My guess is that China will remain basically Maoist for

some time to come. Given the vastly different historical backgrounds of the two countries, it is not likely that China will become another Soviet Union. It will continue to develop along its own lines, and those lines cannot help but reflect the Maoist imprint—the communes, decentralization of industry and planning, the small rural industries, self-reliance, and so on.

VIII. China and the Soviet Union: Development Contrasts[46]

In what ways are China's "lines" different from those of the Soviet Union? Before getting into that, it should be noted that there are many strong similarities between the two countries. Each has a communist party that professes adherence to the general principles and practices of Marxism-Leninism. Each party carried out a land reform shortly after the revolution. Each nationalized industries, collectivized agriculture, and established a national planning system. Each party aimed for rapid industrialization and high growth rates, relying for these mainly on domestic saving for capital formation. Each country has devoted substantial resources to military output. Each party claims to be making significant progress through the stage of Marxian socialism toward communism. Finally, both countries have had broadly similar economic records (see Table 20). Despite these similarities, however, each party has bared its fangs at the other.

Soviet Criticisms of the Chinese

As Soviet critics analyze their neighbor, China's economic backwardness in the initial decades of this century meant inevitably that there would be a preponderance of peasants and small producers who, because of their limited

TABLE 20

CHINA AND USSR: ECONOMIC PERFORMANCES, 1950-1975

(1960 = 100)

	GNP		Industrial Production		Agricultural Production		Population		Primary Energy	
	China[a]	USSR[b]	China[c]	USSR[d]	China[e]	USSR[f]	China[g]	USSR[h]	China[i]	USSR[j]
1950	46	57	15	39	82	66	80	84	22	49
1955	77	76	40	65	121	80	89	92	44	73
1960	100	100	100	100	100	100	100	100	100	100
1965	127	133	111	141	146	115	110	108	90	142
1970	170	170	175	196	165	145	123	113	138	183
1975	232	205	279	263	180	141	137	119	213	240

[a]CIA, Handbook of Economic Statistics, 1976, p. 26, JEC, China: A Reassessment of the Economy, July 10, 1975, p. 23.

[b]CIA, Handbook, p. 28; JEC, China: A Reassessment, p. 23.

[c]CIA, Handbook, p. 26; JEC, China: A Reassessment, p. 23.

[d]CIA, Handbook, p. 26; JEC, Soviet Economic Prospects for the Seventies, June 27, 1973, p. 280.

[e]CIA, Handbook, p. 40; JEC, China: A Reassessment, p. 23.

[f]CIA, Handbook, p. 40; JEC, Soviet Economic Prospects, p. 336.

[g]CIA, Handbook, p. 44; JEC, China: A Reassessment, p. 23.

[h]CIA, Handbook, p. 44; JEC, Soviet Economy, p. 115; JEC, Soviet Economic Prospects, p. 472.

[i]CIA, Handbook, p. 75; CIA, Peoples' Republic of China: Handbook of Economic Indicators, August 1975, p. 15. The first figure is for 1952, the second for 1957.

[j]CIA, Handbook, p. 75; JEC, Soviet Economy, p. 478. The 1950 and 1955 figures may not be comparable to the others. Data are for coal, crude oil, natural gas, and hydroelectric and nuclear electric power expressed in terms of coal equivalents.

238 Economic Development: A Marxist View

daily activities, were incapable of perseverance, organization, and discipline. These petty bourgeois traits were reinforced by China's long isolation from the world. Further, the Soviets claim, the Chinese Communist party (CCP) was driven out of the cities in 1927 and retreated to the countryside. Later, it was forced into the Long March which sent it into even more impoverished rural areas. Thus, the CCP was separated from urban and proletarian currents and became immersed in the regressive and narrow values and outlook of the backward rural areas. To survive without a revolutionary proletariat, the CCP was compelled to establish itself as a military movement. It thus developed into a peasant-based, military-oriented, revolutionary organization that became increasingly bureaucratic in outlook owing to its petty bourgeois origins.

Because of these historical forces, the Soviets say, the CCP has necessarily displayed many deviations from Marxism-Leninism, such as overemphasis on man's "will" and "spiritual power," and on artificial ways of speeding up development and the revolutionary process (i.e., by "leaps," struggles, wars, guerrilla economics, etc.). The CCP also, because of its background, has a fixation on rural areas, agriculture, and small industries, which reduce "the town to the technical level of the countryside." Further, the CCP exaggerates the potency of moral and collective incentives and improperly denigrates technicians and experts—attitudes which come from its glorification of the military, barracks-style of life.

Chinese Criticisms of the Soviets

The Maoists, in turn, have had their say in this battle. The Chinese critics first point to some early difficulties encountered by the Bolsheviks, which compelled them eventually to overstress the productive forces to the neglect of production relations and the superstructure; to

put heavy industry before light industry and agriculture;
investment before consumption; urban before rural areas.
In overemphasizing technology, Stalin had to promote
bourgeois incentives with large wage differentials, piece-
work wage systems, and generous individual bonuses, which
led to marked economic and social inequalities within the
working class. This led to the playing down of class struggles and the rejection of a dialectical outlook. After Stalin's
death, the Maoists claim, Khrushchev and his supporters
usurped party and state power on behalf of a bureaucrat-
monopoly-bourgeoisie that now runs the country as a
fascist dictatorship. This clique no longer believes in class
struggle and revolution and so, accordingly, has espoused
peaceful coexistence with imperialism (belief in the peaceful intentions of imperialism), peaceful transition from
capitalism to socialism (opposition to armed revolution),
peaceful transition from socialism to communism (opposition to dictatorship of the proletariat and to class struggles),
and economism (opposition to bold measures for social
transformation).

The restoration of capitalism in the USSR, according to
the Chinese, has seriously disrupted the development of
Soviet productive forces, and it has opened the door to
graft, theft, depraved social morals, alcoholism and drugs,
and juvenile delinquency. The new capitalist class controls
all monopoly capital in the country and obtains much surplus value through its exploitation of the Soviet and other
working peoples. This is the economic base of Soviet social-
imperialism, the Chinese say, which seeks world hegemony
and "is the most dangerous source of war."

An Evaluation

Despite these diatribes, both countries, as we have seen,
have made substantial economic progress and gains in
equity. Some Marxists believe that China is superior on

both counts, for she appears to have a higher growth rate and to have transformed her relations of production and superstructure more thoroughly to socialist forms than the Soviets have. The thought here is of progress toward full socialist ownership and work relations, the reduction of social and economic inequalities, the diffusion of collective behavior among the population, and the encouragement of mass participation in decisionmaking with consequent improvements in national planning. The Chinese have also shown how social transformation can stimulate technical transformation, with the latter in turn serving as a basis for still further advances in the former. All of this indicates, for some Marxists, substantial progress toward achieving the goals of a communist society, and so they would give the nod to China over the Soviet Union.

However, the harangues from the two sides remind us not so much of actual economic performances as that there is a real conflict between these two socialist giants, which has burdened both countries' budgets with bloated defense expenditures and split and weakened Marxist movements throughout the world, thereby strengthening the capitalist camp. And it is not the only conflict among Marxian countries: Cambodia and Vietnam are fighting, as are Ethiopia and Somalia; Yugoslavia is at odds with several socialist states; China disputes Angola's very existence as a Marxian country; Albania is now feuding not only with China but with the Soviet Union as well; and so on. Economic development in the socialist countries is also taking a variety of forms, some influenced by the Soviets, some by the Chinese, and all by their own national traditions. There is, consequently, much disagreement over what Marxian socialist development is supposed to be. The socialist camp, in other words, is far from united. The more it has expanded, the more it has divided. That, too, is part of our recent experience.

IX. World Views: A Reassessment

The fragmentation of world socialism into contending national states and the many different forms that socialism has taken have important implications for my analysis.

Throughout this paper, I have analyzed economic development within the context of three worlds: advanced capitalism, Marxian socialism, and the LDCs, which are mostly tied economically to the first group. This classification implies a certain view of the world, of the movement of world forces. It implies that I believe the USSR and eastern European countries to be socialist, in the Marxian tradition; that the principal contradiction in the world is that between the socialist and capitalist camps; that there is a Third World more or less separate from the first two; and so on. As a result, my comparisons have been mainly of capitalism against socialism. In this connection, I have suggested that capitalism is not capable of solving the many human problems generated by its mode of production. Indeed, that is the fundamental reason why this has been a century of successful Marxist revolutions against capitalism, and why socialist development of some type (Chinese or Russian or something else) will continue to be the dominant force in world development.

Many orthodox analysts pretend not to have a world political view, the absence of which, they say, shows up in their neutral classification of countries by size of population, amount of per capita income, or geographical location. But these classifications, seemingly neutral, do in fact reflect the political view that nations are all pretty much alike in their basic economic institutions; that they are separate entities, more or less independent of one another; and that they are simply at different points along the one main highway of development destined to be traveled by all nations. If one believes that this is what

the world is like, then, for the LDCs, economic development becomes merely a matter of using tried-and-true
policies to catch up to the countries with a head start. It
is simply a question of poor countries and rich countries,
countries with good starts and countries with bad starts.
I do not believe that, with such a view, one can really understand what is going on in the world.

The Chinese, unlike orthodox economists, do not hide
their political views. However, their vision of world forces
is dramatically different from the one that I presented.
The Chinese allege that there is no longer a socialist camp,
owing to the restoration in the Soviet Union (and in its
satellites) of a form of state-monopoly capitalism.[47] The
Soviet Union, the Chinese say, is now, along with the
United States, an imperialist superpower, and of the two
it is "the more ferocious, the more reckless, the more
treacherous, and the most dangerous source of world
war."[48] This is because the Soviet Union is a highly centralized latecomer, which is rising while the United States
is falling and which relies primarily on military strength
and uses "socialism" to fool the people of the world. Under present conditions, a new world war is inevitable because these two superpowers, which make up the First
World, will contend for world supremacy until one wins.
The central problem in present-day world politics is the
menace that this super-struggle poses to the peoples of
the world and how they are going to resist it.

The Chinese define the Third World as comprising all
the LDCs, capitalist *and* socialist, in Asia, Africa, and
Latin America, including of course China. The countries
and people of this Third World, they say, "constitute the
main force in the worldwide struggle against the hegemonism of the two superpowers and against imperialism and
colonialism."[49]

The Second World consists of the economically advanced satellites of the superpowers—the nations of west-

ern and eastern Europe, Canada, Japan, Australia, New
Zealand, and a few others. These countries, according to
the Chinese, "constitute a force which can be united with
in the struggle against hegemonism."[50]

The implications of China's analysis are that the "true
socialist" countries of the Third World should unite with
the other Third World nations, even including repressive,
right-wing dictatorships such as Brazil, Iran, and South
Korea and that the Third World should seek a unity with
the Second World, even with the main capitalist "enemies,"
such as Germany, Japan, and Britain, all in the principal
interest of combating the aggressive designs of the superpowers, and especially those of the USSR.

So far as socialist development is concerned, China's
analysis seems terribly pessimistic, for it sees socialism as
only a tiny part of the world economy, producing less
than 5 percent of global GNP and only a fraction of that
of the world's industrial output. On the other side, the
superpowers, especially when allied with the Second World,
are in an overwhelmingly dominant position (see Table 21).
The only hope for the further spread of socialism, as defined by China, is a new world war or social revolutions
in the superpowers, the first of which is "inevitable" and
the second quite unlikely. In fact, inasmuch as a dozen
or so countries, in the Chinese view, have recently been
transformed from socialism back to capitalism, a likely
outcome of the present struggle would appear to be the
continued success of capitalism in subverting the few socialist countries still intact. Moreover, capitalism is likely
to be strengthened in those Third World countries that,
in the interest of resisting the superpowers, ally themselves with advanced capitalist countries. A further implication of the Chinese analysis is that the economic decline
of the Second World, instead of being a boon to socialism,
would be disastrous, for it would allow the superpowers
to run rampant among the Third World countries. China,

TABLE 21

THE THREE WORLDS ACCORDING TO THE CHINESE, 1974

Country Grouping	GNP (in 1974 US $ billions)	Population (in millions)	GNP Per Capita[a] (in 1974 US $) Weighted	GNP Per Capita[a] (in 1974 US $) Unweighted	Land Area (thousand square miles)
The Superpowers (2)	2,013 (36%)	464 (12%)	4,338	4,525	12,264 (23%)
The Second World (32)	2,508 (45%)	638 (16%)	3,931	3,956	9,425 (18%)
The Third World (155)	1,015 (18%)	2,789 (72%)	364	964	30,733 (59%)
Socialist countries (8)[b]	264 (5%)	891 (23%)	296	280	4,355 (8%)
All others (147)	751 (13%)	1,898 (49%)	396	1,001	26,378 (51%)
Total or Average	5,536	3,891	1,423	1,508	52,422

Source: *World Bank Atlas*, 1976

[a]The weights are by population.

[b]Includes China, Vietnam, Cambodia, Laos, Korea, Mozambique, Guinea-Bissau, and Albania.

in fact, encourages the countries of the Second World to unify and strengthen themselves. Considering all of this, socialism's future would seem bleak, unless one saw hope in a third world war.

China's analysis has been heatedly challenged from within the socialist camp, particularly by Albania. The Albanians assert that there are four major social contradictions in the world today: (1) between the socialist and capitalist camps; (2) between labor and capital in capitalist countries; (3) between oppressed peoples and imperialism; and (4) between imperialist powers. The Albanians then charge that the Chinese analysis is invalid because it blurs the boundaries between socialism and capitalism, thereby ignoring the fundamental contradiction of the times; it includes proimperialist, reactionary, and fascist forces in "the principal revolutionary force in the world"; it fails to see the main enemy as both (equally) the United States and the USSR; it ignores the major contradictions (2) and (3) in its grouping of countries in the Second World and in its call for unity between the Second and Third worlds; and so on. The Albanians agree with the Chinese that the Soviet Union is a "social-imperialist" superpower, but they part company with the Chinese after that.

The heart of this controversy is whether the Soviet Union is still socialist in the Marxian sense. Because I have already discussed this elsewhere, I will only repeat my conclusions here.[51] In my view, the Soviet Union *is* a socialist country, albeit a bureaucratic and somewhat deformed one that is making little progress toward communism. It conforms to many of Marxism's criteria, including collective ownership, central planning, and much equality within the working class.[52] It also has been strongly shaped by the national traditions from which it grew, by the world conditions at the time of its birth, and by its initial struggles for survival. Its survival, however, made it possible for Marxism to take hold in other countries, which in turn fashioned the conditions that contributed to the still further spread of this movement in "higher forms." Each new socialist arrival, compared to its predecessors, has potentially greater protection against imperialism, more aid from its socialist allies, and wider options among development strategies.

The development of these "higher forms" of Marxism has in turn modified the structure of Soviet society in positive ways. This does not mean that the transition to socialism is irreversible in the Soviet Union or elsewhere, for the old bourgeoisie hangs on, a new bourgeoisie is created by lingering capitalist institutions and practices, bourgeois values that seeped into the consciousness of the working class remain and grow, and all of these subversive elements are supported by the world bourgeoisie. The Soviet Union, therefore, is moved forward by the continuing development of Marxian societies around the world, of which it is itself a vital and integral part, but it is shoved backward by the continuing strength of bourgeois culture both at home and abroad. The tenets of original Marxism continue to coexist with, and stand in opposition to, revisionism in the USSR; this opposition being the ideological reflection of the enduring struggle between the new bourgeoisie and the proletariat. This struggle of opposites has generated both revisionist and revolutionary actions by the Soviet leadership.

So, while the Soviet Union remains in the socialist camp, the outcome of the struggle there between capitalism and socialism is still very much in doubt.

X. Conclusions

Socialist forms of economic development are rapidly replacing capitalist forms. This world transformation to socialism is a fundamental factor affecting all countries in the "three worlds" of advanced capitalism, socialism, and underdeveloped capitalism. It is, for example, responsible for many of the recent economic difficulties of the advanced capitalist countries—a decline in the ability of capitalist classes to draw surplus value from the global system; a consequent retardation of the capital accumulation process, which has caused slower growth and greater unemployment; and increased struggles over shares of national and world incomes, which have led to severe inflationary pressures within the capitalist realm.[53]

The world transformation to socialism is responsible, too, for the growing divisions within the socialist camp. Since this is still the age of fervent nationalism, the spread of socialism is bound to take different national forms, which in turn are likely to come into conflict with each other. While advanced capitalism suffers today from its lessened ability to control world resources and markets and to profit from such control, socialism suffers from its fragmentation.

The world transformation to socialism is partly responsible, finally, for the growing political independence of Third World countries from capitalist-imperialist powers, which has given them more freedom to find their own paths of economic development and to gain control over their own futures. These opportunities, however, are only just now emerging for most of the Third World nations. Since the worldwide struggle between capitalism and socialism will continue to be waged in these underdeveloped areas, Third World countries will be faced increasingly with this choice. One can anticipate intense class struggles within these countries over this basic issue.

As I previously noted, this has been a century of successful Marxist revolutions against world capitalism. There are few signs that this global process has come to an end. It seems to me that socialism is bound to replace capitalism almost everywhere. At the same time, socialism is quite likely to replace even itself—in its earlier, distorted forms.

NOTES

1. The division of countries into "worlds" is as much a political problem as an economic one. Marxists who follow the analysis of the People's Republic of China on this issue would emphatically disagree with my classification. I will discuss this later in this article.

2. The foregoing is taken from my book, *Challengers to Capitalism: Marx, Lenin, and Mao* (San Francisco: San Francisco Book Company, 1976), pp. 142–145.

3. It is commonly agreed that there is an underestimate of the lower income countries' relative income levels. E. E. Hagen believes that, given the incomes of the richest countries, the incomes of the poor countries should be multiplied by 2½ to 3 (and lesser multiples for better-off countries) to bring them into proper relation with standards of living in rich countries. Thus, living standards in the Marxist countries may be on the average of about 40 to 50 percent, and LDCs about 25 percent of those in the advanced capitalist countries. See E. E. Hagen, *The Economics of Development*, rev. ed. (Homewood, Il.: Richard D. Irwin, 1975).

4. Karl Marx, *Capital*, vol. 1 (New York: International Publishers, 1967), p. 13.

5. Paul Baran, *The Political Economy of Growth* (New York: Monthly Review Press, 1957), pp. 141–144, 162.

6. Ibid., p. 194.

7. Ibid., p. 197.

8. International Bank for Reconstruction and Development (IBRD), *Prospects for Developing Countries, 1978–85* (Washington, D.C., November 1977), pp. 7, 44.

9. This measure of self-reliance has also come from the growing dependence of the advanced countries on the raw materials and natural resources of the LDCs. This last, however, has been partially offset by the reverse relationship with respect to food supplies.

10. Michael Todaro, *Economic Development in the Third World* (New York: Longman, 1977), p. 23.

11. Gerald M. Meier, ed., *Leading Issues in Economic Development*, 3rd ed. (New York: Oxford University Press, 1976), pp. 1, 5.

12. IBRD, *Prospects* . . . , pp. 8–9.

13. Hollis Chenery, et al., *Redistribution with Growth* (London: Macmillan, 1975); excerpted in Meier, *Leading* . . . , p. 395.

14. Hans W. Singer, *The Strategy of International Development* (London: Macmillan, 1975); excerpted in Meier, *Leading* . . . , p. 39 p. 395.

15. J. B. Nugent and P. A. Yotopoulos, "What has Orthodox Development Economics learned from Recent Experience?" mimeographed, Food Research Institute, Stanford University, December 1977, p. 1.

16. M. S. Ahluwalia and H. B. Chenery, "The Economic Framework," chapter 2 in Chenery, *Redistribution* . . .; cited in Meier, *Leading* . . .,, pp. 38–43.

17. See, for example, Ahluwalia, "Income Inequality: Some Dimensions of the Problem," *Finance and Development*, September, 1974, pp. 3–7. See also Irma Adelman, "Growth, Income Distribution and Equity-Oriented Development Strategies," *World Development*, February–March, 1975, pp. 70–73, and Hagen, *The Economics* . . . , pp. 228–229.

18. Hagen, *The Economics* . . . , pp. 226–231, discusses these data taken from Chenery, *Redistribution*. . . .

19. Ibid., Actually it would take 130 years.

20. Marx, *Capital*, p. 20.

21. Ibid., pp. 644–645.

22. Ibid., p. 645. My emphasis.

23. These views can be found in Shlomo Avineri, ed., *Karl Marx on Colonialism & Modernization* (New York: Anchor, 1969), pp. 137–139.

24. Baran, *The Political Economy* . . . , pp. 144–150.

25. Ibid.

26. Ibid.

27. A. G. Frank, *Lumpenbourgeoisie and Lumpendevelopment* (New York: Monthly Review Press, 1972), p. 19.

28. This is most fully explored in Arghiri Emmanuel, *Unequal Exchange: A Study of the Imperialism of Trade* (New York: Monthly Review Press, 1976).

29. Samir Amin, *Unequal Development* (New York: Monthly Review Press, 1976), pp. 203, 249–251, 288, 334–364.

30. Karl Marx, "On the Question of Free Trade," in Karl Marx, *The Poverty of Philosophy* (New York: International Publishers, 1969), p. 223.

31. Chenery, *Redistribution*. . . .

32. Hagen, *The Economics* . . . , pp. 53–58.

33. Ibid., pp. 53–54.

34. Strictly speaking, a Marxist-socialist society is one that includes a Marxist-Leninist party that has led the proletariat to power in a revolutionary way, established a dictatorship of the proletariat, and adheres to the principles of proletarian internationalism. It is also a mode of production in which industry is nationalized, agriculture collectivized, and national planning established—all aimed for high growth rates and substantial equality within the working class. Finally, it is a mode of production in which significant progress, through continuing class struggles, is being made toward communism.

The principal features of communism are high labor productivity and classlessness. Progress made in those crucial directions presupposes considerable growth of the productive forces and significant movement toward the elimination of social divisions of labor, of commodity relations, of limited forms of collective ownership of the means of production, of distribution according to work (in favor of need), and of the state and party as class institutions. Progress toward classlessness would also be accompanied by the development of communist individuals, whose morals and values, behavior patterns, and motivations are transformed from bourgeois to communist forms—to selfless behavior, collective motivations, and so on. See my article, "The Dialectics of Development: USSR vs. China," *Modern China*, April, 1978, for further discussion of this.

The 24 countries that I include as Marxist-socialist countries do not all conform exactly to this prescription. A few of them, in fact, have declared themselves to be Marxist in the absence of some important prerequisites. But I accept them if they are well on their way to a stated goal of Marxism.

35. I should note, though, that in the last several years the growth rates of the advanced capitalist countries have declined rather sharply and some of the leading LDCs on the capitalist side have also faltered noticeably. On this score, the capitalist countries now seem to be in more trouble than the Marxist ones. Whatever the comparative trends of capitalism and socialism from 1950 to 1960, capitalism appears to have reached a nodal point in the late 1960s and to have been on the decline since then.

36. Maurice Dobb has many notable contributions in the planning area: See, e.g., *Socialist Planning: Some Problems* (Brooklyn Heights, N.Y.: Beekman, 1970); *Economic Growth and Planning* (New York: Monthly Review Press, 1960); and *Papers on Capitalism, Development and Planning* (New York: International Publishers, 1967). See also Michael Ellman, *Planning Problems in the USSR* (Cambridge: Cambridge University Press, 1973).

37. See Hagen, *The Economics* . . . , pp. 280–331.

38. D. W. Bronson and B. S. Severin, "Soviet Consumer Welfare: The Brezhnev Era," in Joint Economic Committee of Congress (JEC), *Soviet Economic Prospects for the Seventies* (Washington: GPO, June 27, 1973), p. 379.

39. Peter Wiles, *Distribution of Income: East and West* (Amsterdam: North Holland, 1974), p. 25. Quoted in Herbert Block, "Soviet Economic Power Growth—Achievements under Handicaps," in JEC, *Soviet Economy in a New Perspective* (Washington: GPO, October 14, 1976), p. 264.

40. Murray Yanowitch, "The Soviet Income Revolution," in M. Borstein and D. R. Fusfeld, *The Soviet Economy: A Book of Readings* (Homewood: Irwin, 1966), pp. 228–241.

41. See Nicholas R. Lardy, "Regional Growth and Income Distribution: The Chinese Experience," mimeographed, December, 1976; and "Economic Planning and Income Distribution in China," *Current Scene*, November, 1976.

42. Mao Tse-tung, *A Critique of Soviet Economics* (New York: Monthly Review Press, 1977), pp. 51, 93.

43. Ibid., pp. 46, 51, 66, 93, and 141–142. Also *Selected Works of Mao Tse-tung*, vol. 5 (Peking: Foreign Languages Press, 1977), pp. 132, 135–136, 184, 194–195, 239–240, and 246.

44. Mao Tse-tung, *Selected Works . . .* , p. 132.

45. The following is based on my preface to the Japanese edition of *China's Economy and the Maoist Strategy* (Tokyo: 1978).

46. Much of the material in this section is based on my article, "The Dialectics of Development: China vs. the Soviet Union," *Modern China*, April, 1978, pp. 123–156.

47. The Chinese add, regarding the socialist camp, "nor do historical conditions necessitate its formation for a second time," See *Peking Review*, November 4, 1977, p. 17.

48. Ibid., p. 22.

49. Ibid., p. 24.

50. Ibid., p. 29.

51. This discussion is in "The Symposium Papers: Discussion and Comments," *Modern China*,.October, 1977, pp. 443–464, and "The Dialectics of Development . . . ," loc. cit.

52. For definitions of socialism and communism, in the Marxist tradition, see footnote 34 above. Also see Jonathan Arthur, *Socialism in the Soviet Union* (Chicago: Workers Press, 1977).

53. This is discussed in my book, *Challengers to Capitalism*, chap. 6.

Contributors

Arnold C. Harberger is Gustavus F. and Ann M. Swift Distinguished Service Professor and chairman of the Department of Economics at the University of Chicago. He has taught at Johns Hopkins, MIT, Harvard and Princeton as well. But his impact in the development field is not only in his teaching, for he has undertaken specific studies under consultantship arrangements in a large number of foreign countries as well as in the United States. Among these countries are India, Chile, Panama, Colombia, El Salvador, Uruguay, Indonesia, Canada, and Bolivia. He has also consulted with most of the multilateral development agencies. His professional activities are also quite extensive, ranging from the board of editors of the *American Economic Review* and the *Journal of Economic Literature* to the Research Advisory Committee of the Office of Scientific Personnel of the National Academy of Science. His publications continue to deal with questions of efficiency and of social and private rates of return in developing countries.

Celso Furtado is a Brazilian citizen and has worked in a variety of highly important positions in the government of that country. He directed the Brazilian National Development Bank, was a delegate to the Punta del Este Conference in 1961, was superintendent of the Development of the Brazilian Northeast, and in 1962–63, was State Minister for Economic Development. At present he teaches at the University of Paris and has been a visiting professor at Columbia University and the American University. His main work has been in the area of the theory of dependency with reference to Latin America. He has a number of books published in English, perhaps the best known of which is *Economic Development of Latin America.* He has a wide variety of articles published in English as well as Portuguese, Spanish, and French.

Paul P. Streeten has been at the World Bank as a special adviser to the Policy Planning and Program Review Department, working primarily on issues surrounding basic-needs strategies of development. He has taught at Oxford, where he was warden of Queen Elizabeth House and director of the Institute of Commonwealth Studies. He was a professor of economics at the University of Sussex and director of the Institute of Development Studies. He has served as deputy director-general of economic planning of the Ministry of Overseas Development and was a member of the Commonwealth Development Corporation. He is chairman of the editorial board of *World Development* and has published extensively in the development field. His most recent book is *Foreign Investment, Transnationals, and Developing Countries.*

John G. Gurley is professor of economics at Stanford University. His early research was in the area of

monetary economics, and the "Gurley-Shaw" monetary model is widely known. This interest extended
into the development area as he spent time consulting
with the Harvard Development Advisory Service in
Indonesia and with AID in Argentina and South
Korea. His recent work has been on the Chinese
economy and resulted in the book *China's Economy
and the Maoist Strategy*. He has been a senior fellow
at the Brookings Institution, a fellow at the Center
for Advanced Study in the Behavioral Sciences, the
managing editor of the *American Economic Review*,
and the vice president of the American Economics
Association. He delivered the Marshall Lectures at
Cambridge University in 1976.

Kenneth P. Jameson is an associate professor of economics
at the University of Notre Dame. He specializes in
economic development, with particular reference to
Latin America. He has held a Fulbright Lectureship
in Peru and has served as a visiting professor in the
Development Studies Program of the Agency for International Development during 1977. He has worked
as a consultant for the Organization of American
States as well as for AID. He has published a number
of articles, the most recent dealing with models of
"growth and equity" in development.

Charles K. Wilber is presently professor and chairman of
the Department of Economics at the University of
Notre Dame and has taught at Multnomah College
in Oregon, the Catholic University of Puerto Rico,
Trinity College in Washington, D.C., and American
University in Washington, D.C. He has worked for
the Peace Corps and the Interamerican Development
Bank and has lectured before the Agency for International Development and Foreign Service Institute.

Since 1969 he has been an adjunct senior staff associate at the AFL–CIO Labor Studies Center. He is author of *The Soviet Model and Underdeveloped Countries* and *The Political Economy of Development and Underdevelopment* and is working on a book with Professor Kenneth Jameson on the present crisis in the American economy.

Library of Congress Cataloging in Publication Data

Main entry under title:

Directions in economic development.

    1. Economic development—Addresses, essays, lectures.
I. Jameson, Kenneth, 1942-   II. Wilber, Charles K.
HD82.D516   330.9   78-63299
ISBN 0-268-00841-8

Directions in
Economic Development

EDITED BY
Kenneth P. Jameson
and Charles K. Wilber

UNIVERSITY OF NOTRE DAME PRESS
NOTRE DAME - LONDON

Directions in Economic Development